A LANDSCAPE WITH DRAGONS

A LANDSCAPE WITH DRAGONS

The Battle for Your Child's Mind

by Michael D. O'Brien

IGNATIUS PRESS   SAN FRANCISCO

First edition published by
Northern River Press
under the title
*A Landscape with Dragons: Christian and
Pagan Imagination in Children's Literature*

Illustrations by H. J. Ford: pages 58, 66, 79, 92, 109, 131, 167
Albrecht Dürer: title page, frontispiece, 160
Howard Pyle: page 118

Illustrations adapted from
H. J. Ford: pages 16, 26, 42

Eighteenth-century, artist unknown: page 34

Cover art by Howard Pyle
Cover design by Michael D. O'Brien and Riz Boncan Marsella

ISBN 978-0-89870-678-9 (PB)
ISBN 978-1-68149-012-0 (EBOOK)
Library of Congress catalogue number 97–76843
Printed in the United States of America ⊗

For John, Joseph, Mary-Theresa, Elizabeth,
Ben, and Angela,
who taught me how to read.

Then war broke out in the heavens. Michael and his angels waged war upon the dragon. The dragon and his angels fought, but they had not the strength to win, and no foothold was left to them in heaven. So the great dragon was thrown down, the serpent of old that led the whole world astray, whose name is Satan, or the Devil—thrown down to the earth and his angels with him.

Revelation 12:7–11

Dire warnings were come over the land of the Northumbrians and sadly terrified the people. There were tremendous lightnings and fiery dragons were seen flying in the air.

The Anglo Saxon Chronicle, A.D. 793

Contents

Foreword

The last quarter of the twentieth century has witnessed a radical shift in the nature of literature. During previous centuries, as fiction in the Western world wrestled with the issues of life, it always did so from the experience of Christianity. An author may have supported or attacked the faith, but he would always have had to contend with it. That world is now rapidly changing. In the late nineteenth century and with increasing momentum in the early part of this century, a new yet ancient force began to press in to displace Christian principles from the realm of literature. That force is paganism.

A Landscape with Dragons is about the shift in culture from a Christian-based world view to that of a new and revised paganism. The author examines the difference between the two and shows how the pagan message is being packaged to appear as "Christian" writing. But he deals with far more than just the problem of deception. He is examining a major crisis in traditional culture.

O'Brien uses anecdotes from his family life experiences, skillfully woven, insightful, and often amusing. He begins with a story of his own childhood nighttime fears and the wise way in which his mother helped him to overcome them. Having captured our attention, he then explores the fundamental struggle that every person encounters between courage and terror. At this point he introduces us to one of the most helpful subjects covered in the book: the role that fable plays in the development of the imagination and of a healthy world view.

Focusing on Christian fantasy writing, he examines its important effect in the education of children. Choosing three major authors in this genre, J. R. R. Tolkien, C. S. Lewis, and George Mac-Donald, he proceeds to show how the greater body of their writing represents the constructive role that such literature can play in a child's development. He points out, however, a few details of their work in which they deviated—unintentionally, he believes—from the proper employment of symbols. Despite their flaws, they stand in marked contrast to those authors whose misuse of Christian symbols is actually a thin disguise for a deep-seated paganism.

The author is concerned about the growing illiteracy of the Western world. He maintains that, without exposure to a literature springing from authentic spiritual sources, a society will be ill-equipped to detect the influences of false culture. Furthermore, it will be crippled in its effort to establish a healthy culture. O'Brien argues for a return to the traditional role of the fairy tale and for a simultaneous development of new forms of literature. He believes that both movements can recapture the imagination of the present generation and that of generations to come.

The role of symbols is one of O'Brien's central concerns. The symbols employed in traditional storytelling signified real presences in the invisible world, be they angels or devils. They offered spiritual insight into the nature of the Christian cosmos, imparting to the child some essential insights into the invisible realm and the struggle between it and the natural realm where we must live. The book examines one image in particular—the dragon. The author describes how this symbol is common to almost all cultures in some form or other and how in Western literature it has represented the antagonist in a clearly defined battle between good and evil. The battle lines have become blurred because of a growing "religious illiteracy" and departure from traditional use of classical symbols. It is now widely held that dragons are merely misguided, in need of compassion, and in some cases misjudged altogether. The monster is being tamed.

This kind of reversal of symbolism constitutes an invasion of the imagination, undermining our ability to recognize truth. Because of man's vulnerability to the power of impressions, he is becoming less able to grasp reality itself. Good is no longer perceived as good, nor evil as evil; traditional Christian values are considered to be the product of a narrow-minded prejudice. This has led to a blend of human and diabolical concepts in the written word and, more recently, in cinema. A new world view is being propagated, one that attempts to convince the young that demons are friends or cuddly pets and that people can use evil means to achieve "good" ends. The author maintains that the growing confusion that has resulted draws modern man away from traditional Christian spirituality and prepares him to accept occult replacements.

O'Brien goes beyond the written word to examine the power and mechanics of cinema and television and of the video phenomenon that is an offspring of the two. Although he does not dismiss the value of these media, he does make some cautionary notes about the way in which they affect the developing mind of the child and contrasts this with the effects of the written word.

He goes farther into some difficult territory when he addresses the problem of the new genre of films being produced for children. He gives special treatment to one of the most charming of all, the 1993 release of the story of *Aladdin* from Walt Disney Productions. This animated video appears at first glance to qualify as a valid fable according to the principles set forth in this book, but the author provides a thought-provoking insight into the way in which it departs from the traditional role of the fairy tale.

A Landscape with Dragons closes with an essay on Christian "intolerance". The author points out that God was intolerant of our damnation and took it upon himself to remedy it. Our participation in that remedy has certain implications. This closing section serves as a warning cry to a Christian civilization sliding back into paganism.

The result is a book that is always interesting and readable yet, at the same time, deep, powerful, and helpful. A key idea throughout is that there is a line over which healthy Christian culture will not cross. In this collection of essays we are not told where that line is; we are told how to recognize it.

The author does not pretend to cover the subject exhaustively. He does offer some suggestions for further reading, but it seems that his primary goal is to introduce the basic concepts in the hope that they will enable the reader to examine the problem with greater awareness. This landmark work will serve as a stimulus for other authors to explore the subject.

DAVID SLOAN

OTTAWA

Acknowledgments

I am grateful to the many parents who have written to me over the years with insights and questions regarding the battle for our children's minds. I am also indebted to my wife, Sheila, my brother Terry O'Brien, my son John O'Brien, Dr. Robert MacDonald, David and Katherine Jeffrey, and Christopher Corkery for their valuable suggestions. Special thanks to the members of the Bethlehem community of North Dakota for their painstaking labors compiling the booklist that accompanies the text. And last but not least, my heartfelt thanks to Vivian Dudro, intrepid and discerning editor at Ignatius Press.

Chapter I

Encounters with Dragons

An Early Encounter

When I was six or seven years old, I was convinced for a time that a monster lived in my bedroom closet. My younger brother, with whom I slept, was equally convinced, and our attempt to escape into sleep, unnoticed and undevoured, grew increasingly impossible, as did the long walk down the dimly lit hallway to our dark bedroom. We did not mention the problem to our parents because we thought they would dismiss such fears as groundless and (most humiliating of all) babyish! The terror grew in our minds, and one night, finally, we balked in the hallway, clinging to each other in stark fear, and simply refused to go to bed. When the whole story was out, my father bravely stalked down the hallway, beat about in the closet with a stick, and told us that the thing had fled at his coming. We slept well that night, but by the following evening the old dread had returned. My father's patience was growing shorter, but my good and wise mother was inspired with an idea.

She got out colored pens, pencils, and papers and sat us down at the kitchen table.

"What kind of a monster is it?" she asked.

My little brother wasn't exactly sure, but I was.

"A dragon", I said.

"Why don't you draw the dragon."

"No, No, we would be too askaired!"

"It's okay, I'll be right here", she said calmly.

And so we did. I can remember to this day almost forty years later the feeling of intense relief as my pen gave shape to the invisible fear. My imagination went into high gear, and the beast that materialized on the paper was a writhing menace in red ink. It coiled on the white paper; it was an image of chaos and malice, and it liked to eat children.

"Ooh, it is very horrible", said my mother admiringly. And turning to my brother's drawing, she said, "Ah, horrible and evil!"

"Yes, yes", we nodded emphatically.

"Now we will kill it", she said with a confident tone.

She brought some kitchen knives and skewers and handed them over to us. For two little boys who relished the very thought of pocket knives but rarely got their hands on one, this was an amazing turn of events.

"Go ahead", she said, smiling encouragingly.

Even today I can recall the feeling of exultation and relief as we stabbed and tore at the images on the paper. The conquest of the beast went on for some minutes until there was nothing left but a mound of shredded paper. My mother then dressed us in our boots and put on sweaters over our pajamas, and led us out to the backyard in the dark. There was a forty-five-gallon metal barrel out there that we used for burning paper trash. My mother started a fire in it and said that, if we wanted, we could throw the dragons into the fire and burn them up forever. We did so, and as the smoke and flames rose higher, we were all laughing together, and free.

Every person experiences a fundamental struggle between courage and terror. As a child matures, he discovers that he is not omnipotent and indestructible. There are forces out there that are unsympathetic to his essential being. Something in existence is profoundly dangerous. He gradually develops many natural fears that are sensible, for they protect him from physical harm as he internalizes the instructions and warnings of his elders: Don't play with matches, don't run out in traffic, don't dive into shallow water, and so on. The child also develops personal fears that protect his personality from being wounded. As he is taught to treat others with respect, he learns not to abuse, manipulate, or exploit others, and he learns to avoid being the victim of such behavior.

But there are levels of fear that are not so immediately obvious, nor do they appear to be as sensible as the two aforementioned levels. These are frequently called "irrational fears", as if they were completely groundless, when in fact some of them may be well grounded indeed, though not based in the visible world. These I prefer to call metaphysical fears, or cosmic fears, and they are of a spiritual nature. It is a wise parent who recognizes the first awakenings of these mute dreads as the first buds of a spiritual faculty. Of course, some fears that arise from the imagination, such as fear of the dark or fear of being sucked down the drain with the bath water, are entirely groundless. If allowed to grow into obsessions, such fears can result in emotional illness. But I think the greater threat to children today lies in giving too little, rather than too much, attention to so-called imaginary fears. In a seeing-is-believing culture, which denies the existence of the supernatural world, the tendency is to repress all fears of invisible things. But if a child's fear of monsters under the bed or dragons in the closet always are ridiculed as nonsense, his spiritual guard is in danger of being lowered, with the consequence of his becoming more vulnerable to spiritual evil and less sensitive to spiritual good.

Christian parents must keep in mind that their child is an eternal soul, called by God into a world that is a spiritual battleground. As the child grows, his understanding of this struggle develops gradually and at a pace that is appropriate to his individual personality. Children grow best when they are nurtured in an environment that reinforces their sense of security, but this security can be undermined by two apparently opposite parental approaches. On the one hand, we must avoid imparting an overly fearful attitude regarding the nature of the war; but, on the other, we should not pretend to the child that he lives in a perfectly safe world. We should neither inflame nor repress his raw spiritual instincts, but rather we should guide them in the direction of a confident realism. As his awareness of the presence of evil in the world expands, we must help him to overcome his real and imaginary fears with courage based upon faith that God is more powerful than evil. Just as my mother led me and my brother to destroy the dragon, so God leads us forward in battle against the enemy. We do not overcome evil with our own power, of course, but with Christ. Our children's fears provide opportunities to learn this.

The Natural History Museum

When our eldest son was about twenty months old, I took him with me one day to a museum of natural history. He rode happily on my shoulders chattering in his baby language over the displays of birds and monkeys, laughing at the stuffed mastodon, until at last we entered the dinosaur section. There was a sharp intake of breath. I felt his little hands grip my forehead tightly, then he climbed down my body fast and clung trembling to my chest.

"What's the matter, John?" I asked.

He looked up into the jaws of a *Tyrannosaurus rex* and said in a frightened voice, "Eat me."

"What?" I said, completely puzzled.

His face was white and his eyes large. He pointed up toward the dinosaur.

"It eat me."

This was especially puzzling since my wife and I had taken care not to read to him any picture books or stories that contained frightening imagery. We did not own a television set and never watched it when visiting outside the home. No families among our circle of friends and neighbors possessed the new ugly toys that glamorized the horrible and the dangerous. Where could he possibly have gotten the notion that this creature was dangerous and the mastodon was not? (The mastodon, after all, had much bigger teeth.) I filed the incident away in my mind as one of those unexplainable things that I would think about when I got a chance. But family life can be so very, very full, and mental filing cabinets get to spilling over. The question slipped away, unresolved.

A few years later my wife and I suffered through a week of near sleeplessness. Several times a night another of our children, Joseph, aged five, awakened us with a repeated nightmare in which the central character was a malicious reptile. Numerous remedies were applied: hours of consoling hugs, prayers, warm milk, and even rational argument. All to no avail. Again I was puzzled, because he was quite a jolly, secure little fellow and, like the rest of the children, had been fed on gentle stories, exposed to little television and no monster imagery. Wracked with fatigue, I grew increasingly frustrated and made the decision to forbid him further entry to our bed. He would now have to survive in his own little room, which was brightly lit and surrounded by a loving family. We would conquer the irrational, I thought, with an exercise of firm will!

That night, after the decision, I fell into an exhausted sleep. And dreamed. In the dream I walked on a deserted beach beside a vast ocean. With me was the Prince of Wales. We were discussing philosophy when, suddenly, an enormous reptilian beast emerged from the water at our side. This monster was at least sixty feet high, and its eyes glittered with a fervid, evil intelligence. It paid no attention to me but instead spoke to my companion in a low, rumbling voice. Its words were like soft thunder, seducing and flattering the prince, while my whole being was filled with a feeling of horror. The presence of evil was so palpable that I knew even in my dream that it was more than a dream. I shouted at the prince to run, but he could no longer hear. At this point I awoke to find myself in a state of unspeakable terror. With some humor my wife relates how from then on I never refused a child entry to our bed.

Joseph's nightmares tapered off within a week or so and never returned. How the problem was resolved is still not entirely clear to me, but I attribute its resolution to prayer, family affection, and a child's natural growth process. However, the experience had an unexpected side effect, for it introduced my wife and me to an aspect of modern life that we had not paid much attention to until then: A large and growing number of people seem to have been "psychologized", that is, they have developed the habit of analyzing everything about human nature through the flawed magnifying glass of psychology. For them, psychology becomes *the* path to happiness, the overarching perception of reality, the primary category of thought, and in the worst cases an obsession. People who have fallen into this mode of thinking focus on "healing" what they perceive to be "dysfunction" in themselves, their families, and even their neighbors. For example, in discussions with other parents, we were given quite a variety of advice regarding the nightmare problem. I was a little surprised at certain themes that kept recurring in the advice. The child was not handling the problem of "negativity" properly, one suggested. Perhaps in our child-rearing methods we had been too extreme in our emphasis on being "good" and not being "bad". Said another, "Wouldn't it be more balanced if the boy were helped to integrate the dark side?" He needed to "embrace his shadow", said another. I made no comment at the time, but it did strike me as odd the way so many people were beginning to talk about evil as if it were all a great misunderstanding, as if the complexity of the universe could be reduced to the operations of the psyche. We are living in confused times, and the social sciences continuously bombard us with theories of how the human personality grows to a condition of health. Most people invest enormous trust in these theories, a trust that displays elements of religious faith (despite the fact that such theories contain many internal contradictions). And by and large the social sciences are saying that there is no such thing as spiritual evil, and some go so far as to say that there is no objective human good and human evil. They admit that there are social "evils" and social "goods", but they do not admit there are such things as truly evil people and evil forces—certainly not "evil" in the classical understanding of the word. The only real evils, it is now commonly believed, are "social dysfunctions", especially feelings of fear and feelings of guilt.

The True History of the Universe

When our daughter Elizabeth was eight years old, she asked me, "Dad, why did God make dinosaurs?"

An excellent question. I glanced hastily about the room, wishing that someone would write a book titled "How to Answer Children's Unanswerable Theological Questions". We groped around the matter together for awhile, and her questions were really pressing: she wanted to know!

"I mean," she said, "God is good—so why would he make something so scary?"

"Uh, maybe at first God made them to be very big and friendly like whales and elephants, but the devil corrupted the world and changed them from plant-eaters into meat-eaters. Then they started killing . . ."

All the answers seemed to ring hollow. She knew it, and I knew it. I prayed silently. Perhaps it was the Holy Spirit who prompted a thought:

"Elizabeth, I don't really know for sure, but maybe he wanted to make a creature that looked like something we can't see. Maybe somewhere in the universe there's an invisible dinosaur on the loose, and it hates people."

She thought about that for a while. After a few minutes she said, "I get it."

We nodded together, although there was a little faking in Dad's nod, because he was still straining to get it himself.

"Yes," she said, musing, "maybe God wanted to tell us that it can be dangerous here. Like the angels and the devils and all that stuff."

"Yep, maybe like that."

"But the dinosaurs weren't evil, were they?"

"No, not at all. They looked big and mean and ugly, and they were dangerous, but they weren't bad. Same as a snake or a shark isn't bad. They're creatures. And each of them tells a part of a big story. All of creation is like a book with millions of chapters."

"Some are scary, and some are wonderful."

"Right! The dinosaurs are gone now, and the world is full of people, but they left a powerful message for us in the fossils, didn't they?"

"Yes", she said, getting really excited. "And that means we'll never run out of good books to read. There's always a new story."

Yes, I thought, always a new story, but really a very old story. It sounds simple: A king made a beautiful kingdom, and he filled it with creatures whom he loved. A dragon crept out of the darkness and sought to devour an entire world. A brave man faced him, and the dragon slew the man. And the man was God, but nobody knew that until the man came back to life. Then he took the weapon with which the dragon had killed him, and he battled the dragon. The dragon hated the Cross and feared the way the man changed it into a thing that could defeat him and his legions. God is the maker of this one great story, which contains all the billions of lesser stories, and he will decide how the tale ends. This story really happened, and parts of it are still happening and some of the most terrific parts are still to come. If you have the heart of a child, you will know that this is true. And you will know that a certain dragon has a persistent desire to devour our children.

Chapter II

The Shape of Reality—Seeing the True Form

Just a Fairy Story?

Shortly after our children's exposure to dinosaurs, I began to read fairy tales aloud to them. As they listened over the years, they each heard the story on different levels. Interestingly, sometimes a five-year-old could grasp a subtle point an older sibling had missed, yet it was clear that they were all tapping into the mysterious power of Story. I rummaged through attics, library sales, and used-book stores in search of as much old literature as I could find. I even began to plunder the attics and box-rooms of my own imagination, inventing bedtime stories for them. This strained my imagination somewhat, and some of the stories were better than others, but a little goes a long way in a family. The children began to compose their own as well, and there were nights when bedtime became rather an elaborate affair. Telling "pretend" stories naturally stimulated a flow of accounts of real happenings. The children began to regard the day-to-day events of their lives as the material of their stories. Conversation grew; communication expanded. As we developed into a full-blown storytelling family, I noticed something interesting happening in our children's play. First of all, they began to find playing more exciting. Also, they acted out the fundamental dramas of the cosmic struggle between good and evil, embellishing and revising

27

them with startling ingenuity. I gradually came to understand the universal love among all peoples for "fairy stories".

In his masterful essay "On Fairy Stories",[1] J. R. R. Tolkien describes the vital role played by these tales in the cultures of the world. They contain rich spiritual knowledge. The sun may be green and the fish may fly through the air, but however fantastical the imagined world, there is retained in it a faithfulness to the moral order of the actual universe. The metaphors found in the literary characters are not so much random chimeras as they are reflections of our own invisible world, the supernatural. Whether in dreams or conscious imagination, the powers of the mind (and one must see here the powers of the human spirit) are engaged in what Tolkien calls "sub-creation". By this he means that man, reflecting his divine Creator, is endowed with gifts to incarnate invisible realities in forms that make them understandable.

For example, magic has been used traditionally in fairy stories to give a visible form to the invisible spiritual powers. But a crucial distinction must be made between the use of "good magic" and "bad magic" as they appear in fairy stories, because for us in the real world, there is no such thing as good magic, only prayer, the gifts of the Holy Spirit, and abandonment to divine providence. "Good magic" in traditional fairy stories represents these very realities, symbolizing the intervention of God in the lives of good men put to the test. It is actually a metaphor for grace and miracle, the suspension of natural law through an act of spiritual authority, culminating in a reinforced moral order.

Bad magic in traditional stories represents the evil power that the wicked use in order to grasp at what does not rightly belong to them—whether worldly power, wealth, or even love. It is also a metaphor for the intervention of the enemies of God, the evil

---

[1] The essay can be found in J. R. R. Tolkien, *Tree and Leaf* (London: Unwin Paperbacks, 1988).

spirits, in the lives of wicked men. As Saint Paul says, "For we are not contending against flesh and blood, but against the principalities, against the powers, against the world rulers of this present darkness, against the spiritual host of wickedness in the heavenly places" (Ephesians 6:12).

Good magic and bad magic in truthful stories correspond to true religion and false religion in our real world. True religion is the search of the soul for God in order to surrender itself to him, the search for his will in order to fulfill it, the search for truth in order to conform to it. False religion is the inverse. It makes a god out of oneself; it makes one's own will supreme; it attempts to reshape reality to fit one's own desires. True religion is about surrender, while false religion is about control.

Most of us do not learn about the nature of reality through theology, philosophy, or higher mathematics. But all of us readily grasp the language of a parable drawn from the universal human story. The forms may be dressed in elaborate costumes and enact impossible dramas, but they enable the lover of tales to step outside of himself for a brief time to gaze upon his own disguised world. What is the value of this temporary detachment? It is an imaginative withdrawal from the tyranny of the immediate, the flood of words and sensory images that often overwhelm (and just as often limit) our understanding of the real world. A rare objectivity and insight can be imparted regarding this world's struggle for spiritual integrity. In the land of *Faërie*, the reader may see his small battles writ large in the wars of titans or elves and understand for the first time his own worth. He is involved, not in a false or spurious world, but in the sub-creation of a more real world (though obviously not a literal one). I say more real because a good author clears away the rampant undergrowth of details that make up the texture of everyday life, that crowd our minds and blur our vision. He artfully selects and focuses so that we see clearly the hidden shape of reality.

Dragons in Myth, Legend, and Faërie

The term "fairy tale" is used rather loosely, for many of these stories are not about fairies as such but deal with a variety of supernatural beings and imaginative happenings. Ancient hero tales, nursery stories, riddle-songs, legends, myths—all have their place in what is really a very broad field of literature. There are countless tales from hundreds of races and language groups, many dating back thousands of years. With very few exceptions, they display a surprising uniformity in their depiction of good and evil: good is good, and evil is evil.

A rich treasure trove of such fiction grew with the passing of centuries. A pattern of symbols emerged that signified real presences in the invisible world. Beautiful winged persons represented unseen guardians and messenger spirits. At the opposite end of the spectrum, dragons (and a host of other monsters) represented the fiendishly clever spirits that sought man's destruction. These symbols were common to so many races and cultures that they were practically universal. But they were also well suited to the spiritual insights of Christian civilization. The shape of these symbols told the reader in a flash some essential information regarding the invisible realm—a realm that long predated Judeo-Christian civilization and was, even then, a spiritual battleground.

Dragons, for example, appear spontaneously in much of the literature of the ancient world, long before paleontology gave us knowledge of the dinosaurs. Egyptian, Chaldean, Greek, Roman, Aztec, and some Oriental mythologies are full of gargantuan reptiles, and their nature is almost always depicted as malicious and sly. They are frequently associated with "the gods". In the Egyptian religion, Apophis was the great serpent of the realm of darkness, vanquished by the sun god Ra. In Chaldea the goddess Tiamat, symbol of primeval chaos, took the form of a dragon. A close relation exists especially between dragon myths and the mother goddess cults, which explains in part the persistence of human sacrifice in such religions. The dragon god devours human blood and is placated, which is a diabolical reverse image of Christ's sacrifice.

The symbol is not perfectly universal: In some Asian cultures dragons are considered good luck, or at worst a mixture of good and evil. Even Greek and Roman mythology, though it bequeathed ample warnings about the terrifying brood of Medusa, the Gorgons, Hydra, Chimaera, and so forth, did at times regard the dragon serpent as a clever dweller of the inner earth, a knower of secrets, an oracle. This ambiguity is due to the blurred distinctions between good and evil in dualistic Eastern religions and in those early Western cultures influenced to a degree by the East. But in Western civilization, founded on the clearer vision of Judaism and flowering in the fuller revelation of the New Testament, the symbol of the dragon sharpened into focus, assuming its definitive identity. Thus, in the literature of the West dragons have been regarded as powerful agents of evil, guardians of stolen treasure hoards, destroyers of the good and the weak (children, maidens, small idyllic kingdoms), and, on the spiritual level, a personification of Satan prowling through the world seeking the ruin of souls.

Some modern mythologists lamely attempt to explain dragons as an inheritance from the age of dinosaurs, a kind of fossil-memory lingering on in the subconscious. But this theory does not explain why the image of the dragon is so universal when, say, that of the mastodon is not—surely, the prehistoric mammoth would just as deeply impress itself on the mind of primitive man. Neither does the theory explain why there exists alongside the mytho-poetic legends another body of writings that discuss dragon encounters in the factual language of a news report. There are, for example, some forty medieval accounts of encounters with dragons in England. Several of them describe Catholic bishops and missionaries overcoming the dragons by spiritual authority. More frequently the sword is used.

With the rise of Christendom, the slaying of dragons became the crowning achievement of heroes such as Siegmund, Beowulf, Arthur and even Lancelot, the great ideal of medieval chivalry. *Beowulf* was the earliest English epic poem written in the Anglo-Saxon tongue, sometime between the ninth and tenth centuries. It offers a stirring depiction of the battleground and can be read to children once they develop a taste for the heroic style. Through such tales, universal truths entered the world of literary culture and were passed down. If they functioned in some respects like ancient mythology, they were myths with a crucial difference. Actual dragons may or may not have existed, but that is not our main concern here. What is important is that the Christian "myth" of the dragon refers to a being who actually exists and who becomes very much more dangerous to us the less we believe he exists.

Perhaps the worst of the demythologizing in recent literature is the message that the basic stories of the Christian faith, especially the Paschal Mystery, are merely our variation on universal myths. It is suggested that many cultures have tales about a hero who is killed and then returns to life. G. K. Chesterton pointed out, however, that the demythologizer's position really adds up to this: Since a truth has impressed itself deeply in the imagination of a vast number of people of varying times and cultures, therefore it simply cannot be true. The demythologizer does not consider the possibility that people of all times and places may have been informed at a deep, intuitive level of an actual event that would one day take place in history, that would be, in fact, the most important event ever to occur.

The dragon has a vested interest in having us dismiss the account of the battle as make-believe. It is not to his benefit that we, imitating our Lord the King, should take up arms against him. He thinks it better that we do not consider him dangerous. Of course, the well-nourished imagination knows that dragons are not frightening because of fangs, scales, and smoke pouring from nostrils. The imagination fed on truth knows that the serpent is a symbol of hatred and deceit, of evil knowledge and power without conscience. If dragons do exist, it is not in the form of green steam engines or painted Chinese masks or overgrown lizards. The dragon that takes no form is the worst kind, and I would rather it not prowl around the neighborhood I call home. Most of all I do not want it infesting my children's minds. I do not want them befriending it, either, nor do I want it calming their instinctive good fears and perhaps in the process taking possession of their very selves.

At this point I may sound somewhat contradictory. It seems that I do not want dragons in my children's minds, I say, and yet at the same time I want them to read plenty of stories in which there are dragons that act like dragons and meet a dragon's end. In fact there is no contradiction here. It is the real dragon against which I want my children armed. Their interior life has need of the tales that inform them of their danger and instruct them at deep levels about the tactics of their enemy. It is good that our children fear dragons, for in the fearing, they can learn to overcome fear with courage. Dragons cannot be tamed, and it is fatal to enter into dialogue with them. The old stories have taught our children this.

There have actually been suicides brought about through the "Dungeons and Dragons" cult among adolescents. But it is very important to note that this tragedy is not the result of overheating the young imagination with too much make-believe. On the contrary, it is the result of not believing in dragons until it is too late, of thinking it "just a game". It is the logical consequence of our ignorance of this principle: The imagination must be fed good food, or it will become the haunt of monsters.

I do not want our children to grow up believing in the actual presence of dragons. But the child who learns fairy stories knows that flying horses and fire-breathing serpents are not to be confused with the cows in our neighbor's field. Some writers suggest that children do not grasp the meanings in symbol and allegory. This is simply untrue. They may not be able to articulate it in adult terminology, but the young, even the very young, are able to reach across the gap between the real and the sub-created world and find the truths within the mysterious events that are the cosmic drama. They have a natural sense that something mysterious, wonderful, and useful is hidden within the tale, not so much like those trick pictures in which they must find how many bunnies are hidden in the bushes. More like stepping into a marvellous new kingdom where they stand in awe before the fact that angels and dragons are there. The child then asks himself, "Why are they there? And why is it like that?"

Answering the Critics of Fairy Stories

Modern critics of the fairy story have sometimes objected that the world it presents is too simplistic. They maintain that beautiful heroes and heroines are too much aligned with good, and the physically ugly characters are used too much to represent evil. Such an argument is obviously the result of too cursory a glance at fairy tales. There are many stories in which bad characters have a beautiful appearance. There are some in which ugly creatures have noble princes and princesses hidden inside of them. Generally, however, it is true that the exterior forms that many traditional authors give to the morally or spiritually ugly character *tend* to be ugly forms. Likewise, beautiful forms *tend* to express a beautiful interior life. This is a literary device that works well to reinforce the child's budding awareness of interior ugliness and beauty. Children are not so colossally naïve as to think nice-looking people are always nice or that unattractive-looking people are bad. My children know from infancy onward that their grandmother (bad teeth, liverspots, and a big tummy) is the most beautiful person in their life. She loves. She is kind. She listens to them. Also, in their short lives they have met more than one beautiful-looking person who is manipulative, sarcastic, and a user of others. They instinctively dislike such people, for their image is not consistent with their substance. Children know this is how the real world works.

We seem to have lost sight of a keystone that was firmly in place in the culture of classical civilization, one that has been crumbling in the West for a long time and at an accelerated rate since the industrial and the technological revolutions. We have lost our sense of the holiness of beauty, our intuition that at some level it reflects back to him who is perfect Beauty. If a bad character betrays that beauty by sin, this in no way negates the authenticity of beauty. By the same token, when exterior beauty is in harmony with a character's interior beauty, then *the sign value of the tale or the character is greatly enhanced*. Similarly, when worship of God is done poorly, it is not necessarily invalid if the intention of the worshiper is sincere. But when it is done well, it is a greater sign of the coming glory when all things will be restored in Christ. Clearly, God is better glorified by a humble hunchback mumbling badly phrased prayers in a ditch than by a proud aesthete singing hymns perfectly, solely as an art form. Yes, give us that poor, godly hunchback over the vain successful man, rich in his religiosity! But what if the beautiful heart of that hunchback were to dwell in the developed art of the aesthete? Would not a greater glory be rendered to God by the restoration to harmony of both substance and form? In literature we have a medium in which it is possible to express this and, more than that, in which it is possible to show our children that it is possible to live this.

Some modern critics have accused the traditional fairy story of being too fixated on punishment of evil characters. They maintain that children are being conditioned to want revenge, that violent instincts are being incorporated into their personalities, and that they will grow up lacking compassion. Such anxieties stem from the modern preoccupation with peace at all costs, from exaggerated fears about conflict, and from the mistaken belief that sin can be educated out of fallen human nature. Such people believe that children (especially male children) will grow up to be happy nonviolent adults if they are prevented from playing with toy weapons. This is naïve. Little boys deprived of toy swords and guns will simply make their own out of anything that comes to hand (such as Lego, sticks, and even pieces of toast). I draw the line at buying plastic machine guns or bazookas for my children, but I do not consider it unhealthy to spend an hour in the woods with my son finding just the right willow sapling to bend into a bow for him. The principle at stake in this issue is not so much our laudable desires to raise compassionate children. The real question is: What approach will best raise compassionate and courageous children? Normal childhood play, riddled with joys and conflicts as it always has been, "educates" at a profound level. The secret is not to deprive a child of his sword but to make the sword with him and teach him a code of honor. In other words, chivalry. Responsibility. Character. Justice. It is a distinctly modern prejudice that holds that a boy with a sword will probably run it through his little sister. The truth of the matter is, most boys, unless they are mentally disturbed, quickly learn that it is far more heroic, exciting, and rewarding to protect a little sister with that very sword by chasing off dragons and bullies.

Unlike the sword or bow and arrow, the mystique of the *gun* is something of a different problem in the modern era, because it means different things to different people. The word stimulates immediate emotional response in everyone. For those who live in rural areas, where a gun is used for protecting livestock from predators or providing food for one's family, it is like any other useful but dangerous tool. Is it reasonable to propose that we can create a safer world by eliminating references to guns? Can we clean up humanity by sanitizing literature? If so, should we also drop all references to cooking because sometimes an irate house-wife will throw a rolling pin at her husband, or banish references to chain saws because sometimes people have accidents with them when cutting firewood, weed out every reference to auto-mobiles because many people use them badly and even kill oth-ers with them? After all, a far greater number of people die violently as victims of car crashes than die at the wrong end of a gun, or a sword, or a bow and arrow. For the urbanite, however, guns conjure up images of Belfast, Bosnia, gang wars, and high school murders. But this, I believe, has more to do with the power of television than the influence of fairy stories—I suspect that terrorists and drug lords have read very few.

It has been suggested that fairy stories would be much im-proved if they were rewritten without references to weapons, violence, and punishment. Perhaps a few of the Grimm brothers' tales would benefit a little from this, but to apply such "cultural cleansing" to the entire field of children's literature is really a symptom of naïveté about human nature and about the role of literature. The point we must keep in mind is that the fairy story is a *literary* heritage, containing the imperfections that fallen human creators bring to their art. If we were to try to cleanse every work of traces of original sin, we would have to burn a great deal of the literature of the world, and a fair portion of the Bible as well. In the Gospels, for example, Judas does not end well. Neither does Herod, nor a host of odious characters in the Old Testament. "Where is compassion in those texts?" we might ask ourselves, "Where is mercy?" I think the answer, at least in literature, is that stories *teach us*, and this passing on of the truth *is* their chief act of mercy. Part of their task is to warn us, to posit the possibility of damnation. Furthermore, a literary figure is not in fact a suffering person but an image in the mind. And the dire image of a witch's death may suggest in the mind of a child that witchcraft is so absolutely a violation of their souls, of their personhood, that a dire punishment is warranted. Even very young children realize that no one is going to make a witch dance herself to death in red-hot shoes (a cruel and unusual punishment if there ever was one). No, the modern witch will be left very much to do as she pleases—perhaps have an interview on a morning talk show, write a best-selling book, or gather a group of devotees about herself. At worst, she may have to suffer some insensitive comments from her critics.

The fairy story is not an incitement to violence; it is an incitement to reflection on the truth. It does not really propose violence against the sinner (the witch); it reminds us to do violence against the sin (in this case, witchcraft), but more importantly against our own sins, just as the Scriptures command us to do— "If your eye causes you to sin, pluck it out!" The merit of a bad end to a bad fictional character is that it imparts a warning *about the act*. There are worse things than turning into a donkey or dancing to death in red-hot shoes, eternal damnation and diabolical possession being two of them.

The concept of justice is not always easy to grasp, especially in a culture that has been conditioned to exalt rights at the expense of responsibilities, that suffers from the impression that punishment is always a cruel thing. One of law's important functions is to instruct and to deter on an objective level those whose inhumanity (and they will always be with us) impels them toward the ruthless use of other human beings. There is great need for a return to objective warning signs strong enough to prevail over the massive subjectivization of the modern mind—a mind, by the way, that has abandoned the stern messages of right and wrong that one finds in traditional fairy stories; a mind that is instead pumped full of images that glamorize the diabolical. Without clear deterrents, the imagination will soon be influenced by, and eventually infested by, many demons. If that process is not reversed, the malformed mind, pacified by neutered concepts of justice and mercy, will find itself without defenses; it may even in the end come to believe that evil is good, and good is evil.

The purpose of dragons in literature, and of the fascination children have for them, is to arm the soul with an ever-developing discernment of spirits. The purpose of the fairy tale is not to breed superstition but rather to defend the mind against superstition. As I write this I am gazing out the window at an epic being enacted on our hillside. The children are galloping over a yellow carpet of birch leaves on this sunny afternoon, running through the woods with swords they have cut from branches and silver shields they have borrowed from the tops of our trash cans. They are stalking the shadows lurking in the forests and caves. They are armed with homemade bows and arrows, willow rods bent to the breaking point by twine, and wobbly shafts outfitted with chicken feathers and armed with arrowheads they have chipped from stone. Are we training them to be aggressive little militarists? Not at all. They seem rather kind and gentle children, until roused by a real enemy—dragons, for instance.

They do seem to be developing a great deal of character, and it might be important to note here that violent people, on the whole, tend to be lacking in character. The children's play is filled with an implicit moral consciousness of natural and super-natural law, even when, on occasion, they break that law. The point is, they know the law—and the spirit of it.

It is encouraging for us to see how their friends are drawn magnetically to the fantasy life of our young tale-bearers. A community of questers is born on an ordinary Saturday afternoon. For a brief, burning moment they know that nothing is ordinary, least of all themselves. When the moral order of the universe is reinforced, as it is for these children, man begins to know *who* he is, *where* he is, and *what* he is for. When the moral order of the universe is corrupted, his perception of reality itself collapses. The collapse may be slow or rapid, but the end result is a mass submersion into a swamp, in which creation is radically deval-ued, life becomes meaningless, and man, no longer able to know himself, is driven to desperate escape measures.

Chapter III

A Child's Garden of Paganism

Culture and the Search for Truth

Traditionally, the arts of man have been the medium in which his ideas about life are enfleshed, so as to be examined and understood more fully. In practically all cultures throughout human history, art has been intimately allied with religion, asking the great questions about existence:

"What is Man? Who am I? Why am I? Where am I? And where am I going?"

These questions may be expressed overtly or subconsciously, but no one can gaze upon the works of an amazing variety of peoples and civilizations without recognizing that in depictions ranging from the primitive to highly sophisticated, the human soul strains toward an understanding of its ultimate meaning.

Cro-Magnon man crouching in the caves of Lascaux knew that he was something more than just a talking beast, though he would not have been able to articulate this awareness in modern terms. When he smeared charcoal and pigment on the stone walls, depicting the heaving gallop of deer and bison, he was performing a task that has rarely been surpassed for sheer style, beauty, and purity of perception. This is a meeting between the knowable and the mysterious unknown, dramatized in the hunt— one creature wrestling for the life he would extract from the death of another. This is more than a news item about food

gathering. This is more than a tale about filling the stomach. This portrait speaks to us across thousands of years with an immediacy that communicates the rush of adrenaline, terror, exultation, feasting, power, gratitude, and longing. Depicted here is the search for permanence, and also a witness to the incompleteness that greets us again each morning. This is a probing of the sensitive, mysterious roots of life itself. And the little stick men chasing the galloping herds across the wall are a message about where prehistoric man placed himself in the hierarchy of creation. That he could paint his marvellous quarry, that he could thus obtain a mastery over the dangerous miracle, must have been a great joy and a puzzle to him. That he portrayed his quarry as beautiful is another message. The tale is only superficially about an encounter with raw animal power. The artist's deeper tale is about the discovery of the power within himself—man the maker, man the artist! This was not prehistoric man watching primitive television. This was religion.

But primitive religion never stops at the borderlands of mute intuitions about mystery. That mythical figure of the "noble savage" never existed, never was innocent. Because man is fallen and the world inhabited with evil spirits that wrestle for his soul, terror and falsehood have always played central roles in pagan religions. It would be impossible here to attempt even a rough outline of the horrors of early pagan cults, to describe their viciousness, the despair of their sacrificial victims, and their shocking synthesis of all that is dehumanizing and degrading in unredeemed human nature. We need mention only a few of the bloodthirsty deities—Moloch, Baal, Astarte, Quetzalcóatl, for example—to recall how very dark the pagan era was.

Man was created "in the image and likeness of God" (Gen. 1:26). Saint John Damascene once wrote that when man fell, he lost the likeness of God, but he did not lose the image of God. For this reason it remained possible, even before the coming of Christ, for man to search for the truth. Thus, as more complex civilizations arose and language and perceptions expanded, man began to reflect more upon the natural world and upon his own extraordinary nature. A kind of natural theology emerged, building upon what he perceived in the order of creation. In time he began to ask himself if the beauty and harmony he saw everywhere about him were pointing to something much higher than the things available to his senses. Thus was philosophy born—the search for truth, the search for wisdom. And though Greek religion never entirely shook off its "mystical" undercurrents (so similar to Indian mysticism's passion to escape the world of sense and suffering, the bodily existence that it saw as a wheel of torment), it gradually approached a less brutal though still imperfect reading of reality. Through Plato especially, the Greek mind turned away from the intoxicating world of appearance toward an other-world of idealized Forms. These eternal Forms, Plato taught, were the dwelling place of "the very Being with which true knowledge is concerned, the colorless, formless, intangible essence, visible only to the mind, the pilot of the soul" (*Phaedrus*). This was "true Beauty, pure and unalloyed, not clogged with the pollutions of mortality and all the colors and vanities of human life" (*Symposium*). A more idealized, more humane kind of paganism was emerging, though it still contained elements of life-denying escapism.

With only their intellects and imaginations to guide them, the classical Greeks arrived at an understanding that man does not create himself, nor does he create the world around him on which he depends. Life is a gift, and man owes a debt to the mysterious divine power responsible for it. They accepted that man is flawed and incapable of perfecting himself but believed that by adherence to the powers of reason and beauty he could approach the gods and share in their divine life. Thus, Greek art, preoccupied with embodying myths in harmonious forms, was the visual expression of Greek philosophy.

While the classical pagans were gradually coming closer to an approximate understanding of the shape of existence through natural law, God was drawing another people to that truth through pure revelation. The Hebrews, a small, despised race of Semitic nomads fully immersed in the hot spiritual swamps of the East, could not yet avail themselves of the cool northern light of reason. They needed God's direct intervention.

The sacrifice of Isaac was the seminal moment that inaugurated, and the image that represents, the rise of the Western world. It was a radical break with the perceptions of the old age of cultic paganism. When God led Abraham up the mountain of Moriah, he was building upon a well-established cultural pattern. Countless men were going up to the high places all around him and were carrying out their intentions to sacrifice their children. But God led Abraham by another way, through the narrow corridors of his thinking, his presumptions about the nature of reality. This was not a typical pagan, greedy for power, for more sons, or for bigger flocks. This was an old man who by his act of obedience would lose everything. He obeyed. An angel stayed his hand, and a new world began. From then on, step by step, God detached him from his old ways of thinking and led him and recreated him, mind and soul. And thus, by losing everything, he gained all. God promised it. Abraham believed it. Upon this hinges everything that followed.

The Old Testament injunction against graven images was God's long-term method of doing the same thing with a whole people that he had done in a short time with Abraham. Few if any were as pure as Abraham. It took about two thousand years to accomplish this abolition of idolatry, and then only roughly, with a predominance of failure. Idolatry was a very potent addiction. And like all addicts, ancient man thought he could not have life without the very thing that was killing him.

Idolatry tends in the direction of the diabolical because it never really comes to terms with original sin. It acknowledges man's weakness in the face of creation, but it comes up with a solution that is worse than the problem. The idolater does not understand that man is so damaged at a fundamental level that occult power cannot heal him. Magic will not liberate him from his condition. It provides only the illusion of mastery over the unseen forces, the demons and the terrors, fertility and death. Ritual sex and human sacrifice are stolen moments of *power over*, a temporary relief from *submission to*. They are, we know by hindsight, a mimicry of divinity, but pagan man did not know that. He experienced it as power sharing, negotiating with the gods. To placate a god by burning his children on its altars was a potent drug. We who have lived with two thousand years of Christianity have difficulty understanding just how potent. God's absolute position on the matter, his "harshness" in dealing with this universal obsession, is alien to us. We must reread the books of Genesis, Kings, and Chronicles. It is not an edifying portrait of human nature.

When God instructed Moses to raise up the bronze serpent on a staff, promising that all who looked upon it would be healed of serpent bites, he used the best thing at his disposal in an emergency situation, a thing that this half-converted people could easily understand. He tried to teach them that the image itself could not heal them, but by gazing upon it they could focus on its word, its message. The staff represented victory over the serpent, and their faith in the unseen Victor would permit the grace to triumph in their own flesh as well as in their souls. And yet, a few hundred years later we see the God-fearing King Hezekiah destroying Moses' bronze serpent because it had degenerated into a cult object. The people of Israel were worshiping it and sacrificing to it. Falling into deep forgetfulness, they were once again mistaking the message for the One who sent it. The degree to which they were possessed by the tenacious spirit of idolatry is indicated by numerous passages in the Old Testament, but one of the more chilling ones tells of a king of Israel, a descendent of King David's, who had returned to the practice of human sacrifice. The Old Testament injunction against images had to be as radical as it was because ancient man was in many ways a different kind of man from us. That late Western man, post-Christian man, is rapidly descending back into the world of the demonic, complete with human sacrifice on an unprecedented scale, is a warning to us about just how powerful is the impulse to idolatry.

The Incarnation and the Image

Jesus Christ was born into a people barely purified of their idolatry. Through a human womb God came forth into his creation. God revealed an image of himself, but so much more than an image—a *person* with a heart, a mind, a soul, and a face. To our shock and disbelief, it is a human face. It is our own face restored to the original image and likeness of God.

The Old Testament begins with the words, "In the beginning". In the first chapter of John's Gospel are the words of a new genesis.

> In the beginning was the Word,
> and the Word was with God,
> and the Word was God. . . .
> And the Word became flesh
> and dwelt among us.

Here we should note not only the content but the style. The text tells us that Jesus is man and that he is God. But it does so in a form that is beautiful.

Because the Lord had given himself a human face, the old injunction against images could now be reconsidered. Yet it was some time before the New Covenant took hold and began to expand into the world of culture. Jewish Christians were now eating pork and abandoning circumcision. Paul in Athens had claimed for Christ the altar "to the unknown God". Greek Christians were bringing the philosophical mind to bear upon the Christian mysteries. Roman converts were hiding in the catacombs and looking at the little funerary carvings of shepherds, seeing in them the image of the Good Shepherd. Natural theology began to flower into the theology of revelation. Doves, anchors, fish, and Gospel scenes were at first scratched crudely in the marble and mortar, then with more precision. Hints of visual realism evolved in this early graffiti, but it took some generations before these first buds of a visual art blossomed into a flowering culture. That it would do so was inevitable, because the Incarnation was God's radical revelation about his divine purposes in creation. Christianity was the religion of the Eucharist, in which word, image, spirit, and flesh, God and man, are reconciled. It is the Eucharist that recreated the world, and yet for the first two centuries the full implications were compressed, like buried seed, waiting for spring.

When the Edict of Milan (A.D. 313) liberated the Church from the underground, an amazing thing happened: within a few years churches arose all over the civilized world. As that compressed energy was released, the seed burst and flowered and bore fruit with an astonishing luxuriance in art and architecture. The forms were dominated by the figure of Christ, whose image was painted on the interior of church domes—the architectural dome representing the dome of the sky, above which is "the waters of the universe", above which is Paradise. This was no longer the little Roman shepherd boy but a strong Eastern man, dark, bearded, his imperial face set upon a wrestler's neck, his arms circling around the dome to encompass all peoples, to teach and to rule the entire cosmos. He is the "Pantocrator", the Lord reigning over a hierarchical universe, enthroned as its head—one with the Father-Creator and the Holy Spirit. His hands reach out to man in a gesture of absolute love and absolute truth. And on these hands we see the wounds he bears for us.

This is religion. This is art. This is culture. It is a powerful expression of the Christian vision of the very structure of reality itself. Because of the Incarnation, man at last knows his place in the created order of the universe. Man is damaged, but he is a beloved child of the Father. Moreover, creation is good, very good. It is beautiful, suffused with a beauty that reflects back to him who is perfect beauty. It is permeated by grace, the gift of a loving Creator. From this time forward material creation can never again be viewed with the eyes of the old pagan age. It is God's intention that matter is neither to be despised, on the one hand, nor worshiped, on the other. Neither is it to be ignored, suppressed, violated, or escaped. "All creation is groaning in one great act of giving birth", says Saint Paul (Rom. 8:22). Everything is to be transfigured in Christ and restored to the Father. Man especially is to be restored to the original unity that he had "in the beginning".

The New Gnosticism

Man is free to refuse grace. When he does so, he inevitably falls back into sin and error. But because he is a creature of flesh and spirit, he cannot survive long without a spiritual life. For that reason whenever he denies the whole truth of his being, and at the same time rejects the truth of the created order, he must construct his own "vision" to fill the gaping hole within himself. Thus, because the modern era by and large has rejected the

Christian revelation and its moral constraints, we are seeing all around us the collapse back into paganism. There are countless false visions emerging, but among the more beguiling of them is the ancient heresy of Gnosticism, which in our times is enjoying something of a comeback. Its modern manifestation has many names and many variations, including a cold rationalist gnosticism (science without conscience) that claims to have no religious elements whatsoever.[1] But the more cultic manifestations (their many shadings number in the thousands) can be loosely grouped under the title "New Age Movement". In order to understand its power over the modern mind we need to examine its roots in ancient Gnosticism.

Gnostic cults predate Christianity, having their sources in Babylonian, Persian, and other Eastern religions, but they spread steadily throughout the Middle East and parts of Europe, coming to prominence during the second century A.D. By the latter half of the third century, their power was in sharp decline, due in no small part to the influence of the teachings of the early Church Fathers, notably Saint Irenaeus. Irenaeus links the Gnostics to the influence of the magician Simon Magus, mentioned in Acts 8:9, where Saint Luke says that Simon "used sorcery, and bewitched the people of Samaria". This same Simon offered money to the apostles in an attempt to buy the power of the Holy Spirit. When he was rebuked by Peter, he apparently repented, but second-century sources say that his repentance was short-lived

[1] This is a false claim, because some scientific theories exhibit the qualities of religious myth and function that way in the thought of many supposedly objective minds. For those interested in learning more about this trend, I suggest five scholarly studies: Eric Voegelin's *Science, Politics, and Gnosticism* and his *The New Science of Politics*, Thomas Molnar's *The New Paganism*, Wolfgang Smith's *Cosmos and Transcendence* and his *Teilhardism and the New Religion*. While all these books are a useful contribution to the study of Gnosticism, they are not of equal merit. The latter two titles are unencumbered by certain presumptions that mar the first three.

and that he persisted in the practice of magic. Early Church writers refer to him as the first heretic; Irenaeus and others call him the father of Gnosticism.[2]

The Gnostics continued to have influence until the eighth century and never entirely disappeared from the life of the Western world. Strong traces of Gnosticism can be found in the great heresies that plagued the early Church, in Manichaenism (a cult to which Saint Augustine belonged before his conversion), in kabbalism, medieval witchcraft, occult sects, Theosophy, Freemasonry, and offshoots of the latter.

Gnosticism was in essence syncretistic, borrowing elements from various pagan mystery religions. Its beliefs were often wildly contradictory. For example, some Gnostic groups were pantheistic (worshiping nature as divine), and others, the majority, were more strongly influenced by Oriental dualism (that is, the belief that material creation is evil and the divine realm is good). Despite these confusing differences, they shared in common the belief that knowledge (from the Greek word *gnosis*) was the true saving force. Secret knowledge about the nature of the universe and about the origin and destiny of man would release a "divine spark" within certain enlightened souls and unite them to some distant, unknowable Supreme Being. This Being, they believed, had created the world through Seven Powers, sometimes called the Demiurge. The initiate in the secret knowledge possessed a kind of spiritual map that would guide him to the highest heaven, enabling the soul to navigate the realms of the powers, the demons, and the deities who opposed his ascent. If the initiate could master their names, repeat the magic formulas and rituals, he would by such knowledge (and sheer force of his will) penetrate to the realm of ultimate light.

[2] See *A Dictionary of Biblical Tradition in English Literature*, ed. David Lyle Jeffrey (Grand Rapids, Mich.: Eerdmans, 1992), p. 714.

Superficially, Gnosticism resembles the Christian doctrine of salvation, but the spirit of Gnosticism is utterly alien to Christianity. The two are fundamentally different in their understanding of God, man's identity, and the nature of salvation. Cultic *gnosis* was not, in fact, a pursuit of knowledge as such; it was not an intellectual or scientific pursuit, but rather a supposed "revelation" of hidden mysteries that could be understood only by a superior class of the enlightened. In a word, it was "mystical". But this mysticism could never come to terms with material creation in the way the Christian faith had. Even the "Christian" Gnostics found it impossible to reconcile their concept of salvation with a historical redeemer, nor could they accept the resurrection of the body. They could only attempt a crude grafting of the figure of Christ into their mythology. In their thinking, Jesus was no more than a divine messenger who brought gnosis in a disguised, symbolic form to simple-minded Christians. The Gnostic Gospel, they believed, was the unveiling of the higher meaning. They were the first perpetrators of the idea that "all religions are merely misunderstood mythologies"—a catchphrase that in our own times has hooked large numbers of New Age devotees, agnostics, and even some naïve Christians.

G. K. Chesterton, who was involved briefly with the occult during his youth and later became one of this century's greatest apologists for the faith, understood the powerful seductions of counterfeit religion. The new heretics, he maintained, were not for the most part purveyors of bizarre sects; they were rather fugitives from a decaying Protestant liberalism or victims of the inroads made by Modernism into the Catholic Church. They were groping about in the dark trying to strike lights from their own supposed "divine spark", and the effort could appear heroic. The exaltation of the rebel against organized religion, Chesterton knew, was really a romantic illusion. At the time he wrote his book *Heretics* (published in 1905), the illusion did not appear to be a widespread evil, but he foresaw that it would be the breeding ground for an apostasy that would spread throughout the entire Western world. Each succeeding generation would be fed by a large and growing cast of leading cultural figures who rejected Christianity and made disbelief credible, even admirable. Chesterton understood that culture is a primary instrument of forming a people's concept of reality. And he warned that when shapers of culture slough off authentic faith, they are by no means freed to be objective. They merely open themselves to old and revamped mythologies. When men cease to believe in God, he observed, they do not then believe in nothing; they will then believe in anything.

Chesterton prophesied that the last and greatest battles of civilization would be fought against the religious doctrines of the East. This was an odd prophecy, because at the time the influence of both Hinduism and Buddhism was minor, and devotees of the European occult movements were few in number. Yet within a century we find a great many people in the arts, the universities, the communications media, psychology, and other "social sciences" exhibiting strong attraction to, and promoting pagan concepts of, the cosmos. During the past three decades these ideas have flowed with great force into the mainstream of Western culture, surfacing in all aspects of life and even invading Catholic spirituality. One now sees among professed religious, clerics, educators, and lay people a persistent fascination with Jungian psychology, which is based in no small part on Hinduism and ancient Gnosticism. Those who are in doubt of this should read Carl Jung's autobiography, *Memories, Dreams, Reflections*, which includes a section of Gnostic reflections titled "Seven Sermons to the Dead", written when he was in his early forties. Consider also the following passage from his later work *The Practice of Psychotherapy*: "The unconscious is not just evil by nature, it is also the source of the highest good: not only dark but also light, not only bestial, semihuman and demonic, but superhuman, spiritual, and in the classical sense of the word, 'divine'." That Christians give this pseudo-scientific theorizing credibility is symptomatic of grave spiritual confusion. We should not be surprised that many people immersed in Jungianism are also attracted to astrology, Enneagrams, and other "mystical" paths that promise self-discovery and enlightenment. That large numbers of Christians now seem unable to see the contradiction between these concepts and ortho-dox Christianity is an ominous sign. The new syncretism has been romanticized as the heroic quest for ultimate healing, ultimate unity, ultimate light—in other words, esoteric "knowledge" as salvation.[3]

Many Christians are becoming Gnostics without realizing it. Falling to the primeval temptation in the garden of Eden: "You shall be as gods, knowing good and evil", they succumb to the desire for godlike powers, deciding for themselves what is good and what is evil. The error of Gnosticism is that knowledge can be obtained and used to perfect oneself while circumventing the authority of Christ and his Church. Using a marketing tech-nique that proves endlessly productive, Satan always packages this offer with the original deception, by proclaiming that God and the Church do not want man to have knowledge because it will threaten their power and by asserting that God is a liar ("You will not die"). Authentic Christianity has no quarrel with genuine science, with the pursuit of knowledge for good ends. But because the Church must maintain the whole truth about man, she warns that unless the pursuit of knowledge is in sub-mission to the pursuit of wisdom, it will not lead to good; if it is divorced from God's law, it will lead to death.

A people cut off from true spiritual vision is condemned to a desolation in which eventually any false spiritual vision will

[3] Readers who wish to learn more about this tragic development should read Fr. Mitchell Pacwa's *Catholics and the New Age* (Ann Arbor, Mich.: Servant Pub-lications, 1992).

appear religious. Man cannot live long without a spiritual life. Robbed of his own story, he will now listen to any lie that is spun in a flattering tale. This is one of the long-term effects of undermining our world of symbols. It is one of the effects of assuming that ideas are mere abstractions—a very dangerous misconception, as the tragic events of our century have proved so often.

Recently, a young artist showed me her new paintings. She is an intelligent and gifted person, and the work was of high quality, visually beautiful. With particular pleasure she pointed out a painting of a woman with dozens of snakes wriggling in her womb. It was a self-portrait, the artist explained. Judaism and Christianity, she went on to say, had unjustly maligned the serpent. And in order to rehabilitate this symbol, it was necessary to take the serpent into her womb, to gestate it, and eventually to bear it into the world as a "sacred feminine icon". I pointed out that the meanings of symbols are not merely the capricious choices of a limited culture. We cannot arbitrarily rearrange them like so much furniture in the living room of the psyche. To tamper with these fundamental types is spiritually and psychologically dangerous because they are keystones in the very structure of the mind. They are a language about the nature of good and evil; furthermore, they are points of contact with these two realities. To face evil without the spiritual equipment Christianity has given us is to put oneself in grave danger. But my arguments were useless. She had heard a more interesting story from a famous "theologian".

This is one of the results of forgetting our past. The record of salvation history in the Old Testament is primarily about the Lord's effort to wean man of idolatry and to form a people capable of receiving the revelation of Jesus Christ. It was a long, painfully slow process marked by brilliant moments and repeated backslides into paganism. It bears repeating: when Hezekiah inherited the throne, smashed the pagan shrines, and broke up the bronze serpent that Moses had made, the people of God had for centuries already seen abundant evidence of God's authority and power. What had happened to them? Why did they have such short memories? Was Hezekiah overreacting? Was this a case of alarmism? Paranoia, perhaps? The bronze serpent, after all, had been made at God's command. Hezekiah's act must be understood in the context of the fierce grip that the spirit of idolatry had over the whole world. The people had succumbed to the temptation to blend biblical faith with pagan spirituality. They had forgotten the lesson learned by their ancestors in the exodus from Egypt:

> When the savage rage of wild animals
> overtook them,
> and they were perishing from the bites of writhing snakes,
> your wrath did not continue to the end.
> It was by way of reprimand, lasting a short time,
> that they were distressed,
> for they had a saving token to remind them of the
> commandment of your Law.
> Whoever turned to it was saved,
> not by what he looked at,
> but by you, the universal savior. . . .
> And by such means you proved to our enemies
> that it is you who deliver from every evil. . . .
> For your sons, not even the fangs of venomous
> serpents could bring them down;
> your mercy came to their help and cured them. . . .
> One sting—how quickly healed!—to remind them of your
> utterances,
> rather than, sinking into deep forgetfulness,
> they should be cut off from your kindness.
>
> Wisdom 16: 5–12

What has happened to the people of our times? Why do *we* have such short memories? It is because over-familiarity and the passage of time blur the sharp edges of reality. Minds and hearts grow lax. Vigilance declines. Again and again man sinks into deep forgetfulness. Serpents and dragons are now tamed like pets by some, worshiped by others. The writer of the book of Revelation has something to say about this. He reminds us with a note of urgency that we are in a war zone. Every human soul is in peril; our every act has moral significance. Our danger increases to the degree that we do not understand the nature of our enemy. Saint John wrote us a tale drawn from a vision of what will come to pass on this earth and in our Church. It was given in a form that can be imparted to the soul of a child or to those who have become as little children, but not in a form that can be mastered by those who fail to approach it with reverence. In chapter 12, John tells us that a dragon has a passion to devour our child:

> A great sign appeared in the sky, a woman clothed with the sun, with the moon under her feet, and on her head a crown of twelve stars. Because she was with child, she cried aloud in pain as she labored to give birth. Then another sign appeared in the sky: it was a huge dragon, flaming red, with seven heads and ten horns; on his head were seven crowns. His tail swept a third of the stars from the sky and hurled them down to the earth. Then the dragon stood before the woman about to give birth, ready to devour her child as soon as it was born.

The early Church Fathers taught that this passage has a twofold meaning: on one level it refers to the birth of Christ; on another it refers to the Church as she labors to bear salvation into the world. This child is, in a sense, every child. The Church is to carry this child as the image of God, transfigured in Christ, and to bring him forth into eternal life. She groans in agony, and the primeval serpent hates her, for he knows that her offspring, protected and grown in her womb, will crush his head.

Chapter IV

The Mortal Foe of My Children

The New Illiteracy

Like it or not, we are fast becoming an illiterate people. Yes, most of us can read. Indeed, adults and children now read more books, numerically speaking, than at any other time in history. But our minds are becoming increasingly passive and image oriented because of the tremendous influence of the visual media. Television, film, and the video revolution dominate our culture like nothing before in the history of mankind. In addition, computers, word processors, pocket calculators, telephones, and a host of similar inventions have lessened the need for the disciplines of the mind that in former generations were the distinguishing marks of an intelligent person. In those days man learned to read and write because of necessity or privilege: maps, medical lore, the history of the race, genealogies, and recipes. Each of these could be handed down intact to the forthcoming generations far more easily, and with greater accuracy, in written form than by word of mouth.

So too with the ancient myths and legends that embodied the spiritual intuitions of a people. The printed word guaranteed that no essential detail would be lost. And if the storyteller had the soul of an artist, he could also impart the flavor of his times, the spiritual climate in which his small and large dramas were enacted. Words made permanent on a page would to some extent overcome the weaknesses of memory and avoid the constant tendency in human nature to distort and to select according to tastes and prejudices. Furthermore, the incredible act of mastering a written language greatly increased a person's capacity for clear thought. And people capable of thought were also better able—at least in theory—to avoid the mistakes of their ancestors and to make a more humane world. The higher goal of literacy was the ability to recognize truth and to live according to it.

Something is happening in modern culture that is unprecedented in human history. At the same time that the skills of the mind, especially the power of discernment, are weakened, many of the symbols of the Western world are being turned topsy-turvy. This is quite unlike what happened to the pagan faiths of the ancient classical world with the gradual fading of their mythologies as their civilizations developed. That was a centuries-long draining away of the power and meaning of certain mythological symbols. How many Greeks in the late classical period, for example, truly believed that Zeus ruled the world from Mount Olympus? How many citizens of imperial Rome believed that Neptune literally controlled the oceans? In Greece the decline of cultic paganism occurred as the Greeks advanced in pursuit of truth through philosophy. For many Greeks the gods came to be understood as personifications of ideals or principles in the universe. The Romans, on the other hand, grew increasingly humanistic and materialistic. Though the mystery cults of the East flooded into the West as the Empire spread, the Roman ethos maintained more or less a basic pragmatism; at its best it pursued the common good, civic order, philosophical reflection. At its worst it was superstitious and unspeakably cruel. But all of this was a long, slow process of development, inculturation, and decline.

By contrast, the loss of our world of symbols is the result of a deliberate attack upon truth, and this loss is occurring with astonishing rapidity. On practically every level of culture, good is no longer presented as good but rather as a prejudice held by a limited religious system (Christianity). Neither is evil any longer perceived as evil in the way we once understood it. Evil is increasingly depicted as a means to achieve good.

With television in most homes throughout the Western world, images bombard our minds in a way never before seen. Children are especially vulnerable to the power of images, precisely because they are at a stage of development when their fundamental concepts of reality are being formed. Their perceptions and understanding are being shaped at every moment, as they have been in every generation, through a ceaseless ingathering of words and images. But in a culture that deliberately targets the senses and overwhelms them, employing all the genius of technology and art, children have fewer resources to discern rightly than at any other time in history. Flooded with a vast array of entertaining stimuli, children and parents suppose that they live in a world of multiple choices. In fact, their choices are shrinking steadily, because as the quantity increases, quality decreases. Our society is the first in history to produce such a culture and to export it to the world, sweeping away the cultures of various nations, peoples, and races and establishing the world's first global civilization. But what is the character of this new civilization?

The modern mind is no longer formed on a foundation of absolute truths, which past societies found written in the natural law and which were revealed to us more explicitly in Christianity. At one time song and story handed down this world of insight from generation to generation. But our songs and stories are being usurped. Films, videos, and commercial television have come close to replacing the Church, the arts, and the university as the primary shaper of the modern sense of reality. Most children now drink from these polluted wells, which seem uncleanable and unaccountable to anyone except the money-makers. The children who do not drink from them can feel alienated from their own generation, because they have less talk and play to share with friends who have been fed only on the new electronic tales.

Busy modern parents seem to have less time to read to their children or to tell them stories. Many children grow up never having heard a nursery rhyme, not to mention a real fairy tale, legend, or myth. Instead, hours of their formative years are spent watching electronic entertainment. The sad result is that many children are being robbed of vital energies, the native powers of the imagination replaced by an addict's appetite for visceral stimuli, and creative play replaced with lots of expensive toys that are the spinoffs of the shows they watch. Such toys stifle imaginative and creative development because they do practically everything for the child, turning him into the plaything of market strategists. Moreover, most media role models are far from wholesome. Dr. Brandon Centerwall, writing in the June 10, 1992, issue of the *Journal of the American Medical Association,* links television violence with the soaring crime rates. There would be ten thousand fewer murders, seventy thousand fewer rapes, and seven hundred thousand fewer violent assaults, he says, if television had never been invented.

Many parents exercise very little control over their children's consumption of entertainment. For those who try to regulate the tube, there is a constant struggle. A parent may stand guard by the television set, ready to turn it off or change the channel if offensive material flashes across the screen, but he will not be quick enough. Immoral or grotesque scenes can be implanted in his children's minds before he has a chance to flick the remote control. He may even fall victim to his own fascination and lose the will to do so. Scientific studies have shown conclusively that within thirty seconds of watching television, a viewer enters a measurable trancelike state. This allows the material shown to bypass the critical faculty, so that images and ideas are absorbed by the mind without conscious reflection. Even when the contents of a program are not grossly objectionable, hours of boredom and nonsense are tolerated, because the viewer keeps hoping insanely that the show will get better. Television beguiles many of the senses at once, and the viewer is locked into its pace in order not to "miss anything".

But perhaps the shows ought to be missed. When one listens carefully to many of the programs made for children, one frequently hears the strains of modern Gnosticism: "If you watch this, you will know more, be more grown-up, more smart, more cool, more funny, more able to talk about it with your friends." —"You decide. You choose. Truth is what you believe it to be." — "Right and wrong are what you feel are right and wrong for you. Question authority. To become what you want to be, you must be a rebel."—"You make yourself; you create your own reality."—"We can make a perfect world. Backward older people, especially ignorant traditionalists, are the major stumbling blocks to building a peaceful, healthy, happy planet." And so forth. It's all there in children's culture, and it pours into their minds with unrelenting persistence, sometimes as the undercurrent but increasingly as the overt, central message. What stands in the path of this juggernaut? What contradicts these falsehoods? Parental authority? The Church? In film after film parents (especially fathers) are depicted as abusers at worst, bumbling fools at best. Christians are depicted as vicious bigots, and ministers of religion as either corrupt hypocrites or confused clowns.

The young "heroes" and "heroines" of these dramas are the mouthpieces of the ideologies of modern social and political movements, champions of materialism, sexual libertarianism, environmentalism, feminism, globalism, monism, and all the other isms that are basically about reshaping reality to fit the new world envisioned by the intellectual élites. Victims of their own gnosis (which they see in grand terms of "broadness" of vision, freedom, and creativity), they are in fact reducing the mystery and majesty of creation to a kind of Flatland. If this were a matter of simple propaganda, it would not get very far. No one can survive long in Flatland, because at root it is busy demolishing the whole truth about man, negating the ultimate worth of the human person, and turning him into an object to be consumed or manipulated. Thus, the propagandist must prevent any awakening of conscience and derail the development of real imagination in his audience. He must inflame the imagination in all the wrong directions and supply a steady dose of pleasurable stimuli as a reward mechanism. He must calm any uneasiness in the conscience by supplying many social projects, causes, and issues that the young can embrace with passionate pseudo-idealism.

The late Dr. Russell Kirk, in a lecture on the moral imagination, warned that a people who reject the right order of the soul and the true good of society will in the end inherit "fire and slaughter". When culture is deprived of moral vision, the rise of the "diabolic imagination" is the inevitable result. What begins as rootless idealism soon passes into the sphere of "narcotic illusions", then ends in "diabolic regimes".[1] Tyrants come in many forms, and only the ones who inflict painful indignities on us are immediately recognizable for what they are. But what happens to the discernment of a people when a tyrant arrives without any of the sinister costumes of brutal dictators? What happens when the errors come in pleasing disguises and are promoted by talented people who know full well how to use all the resources of modern psychology to make of the human imagination the instrument of their purpose? How long will it take the people of our times to understand that when humanist sentiments replace

[1] Russell Kirk, "The Perversity of Recent Fiction: Reflections on the Moral Imagination", in *Reclaiming a Patrimony* (Washington, D.C.: The Heritage Foundation, 1982).

moral absolutes, it is not long before we see idealists corrupting conscience in the name of liberty and destroying human lives in the name of humanity?

In many ways this new visual culture is pleasurable, but it is a tyrant. Literature, on the other hand, is democratic. One can pause and put a book down and debate with the author. One can take it up later, after there has been time to think or do some research. The reader's imagination can select what it wishes to focus on, whereas in electronic visual media the mind is pummeled with powerful stimuli that bypass conscious and subconscious defenses. It is tragic, therefore, that authentic literature is slowly disappearing from public and school libraries and being replaced by a tidal wave of children's books written by people who appear to have been convinced by cultic psychology or converted in part or whole by the neopagan cosmos. Significantly, their use of language is much closer to the operations of electronic culture, and their stories far more visual than the thoughtfull fiction of the past. They are evangelists of a religion that they deny is a religion. Yet, in the new juvenile literature there is a relentless preoccupation with spiritual powers, with the occult, with perceptions of good and evil that are almost always blurred and at times downright inverted. At least in the old days dragons looked and acted like dragons. This, I think, not only reflects truth in a deep spiritual sense, it is also a lot more interesting. A landscape with dragons is seldom boring.

Invasion of the Imagination

The invasion of our children's imagination has two major fronts. The first is the degradation of the human image. The second is the corruption of conscience. The territory of fantasy writing, for example, which was once concerned with a wholesome examination of man's place in the cosmos, has become almost without

our knowing it a den of vipers. The genre has been nearly overwhelmed by the cult of horror. A new wave of grisly films and
novels is preoccupied with pushing back boundaries that would
have been intolerable a generation ago. The young are its first
victims, because they are naturally drawn to fantasy, finding in
the genre a fitting arena for their sense of the mystery and danger of human existence. Yet the arena has been filled with demonic
forms and every conceivable monster of the subconscious, all
intent, it appears, on mutilating the bodies, minds, and spirits of
the dramatic characters.

The novels of R. L. Stine, for example, have practically taken
over the field of young adult literature in recent years. Since
1988, when the first title of his *Fear Street* series was released, and

1992, when the *Goosebumps* series appeared, more than a hundred million copies of his books have made their way into young hands. Through school book clubs, libraries, and book racks in retail outlets ranging from department stores to pharmacies, an estimated one and a quarter million children are introduced to his novels every month. For sheer perversity these tales rival anything that has been published to date. Each is brimming over with murder, grotesque scenes of horror, terror, mutilation (liberally seasoned with gobbets and gobbets of blood and gore). Shock after shock pummels the reader's mind, and the child experiences them as both psychological and physical stimuli. These shocks are presented as ends in themselves, raw violence as entertainment. In sharp contrast, the momentary horrors that occur in classical tales always have a higher purpose; they are intended to underline the necessity of courage, ingenuity, and character; the tales are about brave young people struggling through adversity to moments of illumination, truth, and maturity; they emphatically demonstrate that good is far more powerful than evil. Not so with the new wave of shock-fiction. Its "heroes" and "heroines" are usually rude, selfish, sometimes clever (but in no way wise), and they never grow up. This nasty little world offers a thrill per minute, but it is a like a sealed room from which the oxygen is slowly removed, replaced by an atmosphere of nightmare and a sense that the forces of evil are nearly omnipotent.

Stine does not descend to the level of dragging sexual activity into the picture, as do so many of his contemporaries. He doesn't have to; he has already won the field. He leaves some room for authors who wish to exploit the market with other strategies. Most new fiction for young adults glamorizes sexual sin and psychic powers and offers them as antidotes to evil. In the classical fairy tale, good wins out in the end and evil is punished. Not so in many a modern tale, where the nature of good and evil is redefined: it is now common for heroes to employ evil to defeat evil, despite the fact that in the created and sub-created order this actually means self-defeat.

In the *Dune* series of fantasy novels, for example, a handsome, young, dark prince (the "good guy") is pitted against an antagonist who is the personification of vice. This "bad guy" is so completely loathsome physically and morally (murder, torture, and sexual violence are among his pastimes) that by contrast the dark prince looks like an angel of light. The prince is addicted to psychedelic drugs and occult powers, both of which enhance his ability to defeat his grossly evil rival. He is also the master of gigantic carnivorous worms (it may be worth recalling here that "worm" is one of several medieval terms for a dragon). There is a keen intelligence behind the *Dune* novels and the film that grew out of them. The author's mind is religious in its vision, and he employs a tactic frequently used by Satan in his attempt to influence human affairs. He sets up a horrible evil, repulsive to everyone, even to the most naïve of people. Then he brings against it a lesser evil that has the appearance of virtue. The people settle for the lesser evil, thinking they have been "saved", when all the while it was the lesser evil that the devil wished to establish in the first place. Evils that appear good are far more destructive in the long run than those that appear with horns, fangs, and drooling green saliva.

The distinction may not always be clear even to discerning parents. Consider, for example, another group of fantasy films, the enormously successful *Star Wars* series, the first of which was released in 1977, followed by two sequels. They are the creation of a cinematic genius, so gripping and so thoroughly enjoyable that they are almost impossible to resist. The shining central character, Luke Skywalker, is so much a "good guy" that his heroic fight against a host of evil adversaries resembles the battles of medieval knights. Indeed, he is called a "knight", though not one consecrated to chivalry and the defense of Christendom, but one schooled in an ancient mystery religion. He too uses supernatural powers to defeat the lower forms of evil, various repulsive personifications of vice. Eventually he confronts the "Emperor", who is a personification of spiritual evil. Both Luke and the emperor and various other characters tap into a cosmic, impersonal power they call "the Force", the divine energy that runs the universe. There is a "light side of the Force" and a "dark side of the Force". The force is neither good nor evil in itself but becomes so according to who uses it and how it is used.

There is much to recommend this film trilogy, such as its message that good does win out over evil if one perseveres with courage. The romantic side of the plot is low-key and handled with surprising sensitivity to the real meaning of love (with the exception of two brief scenes). Other messages: The characters are unambiguously on the side of good or evil; even the one anti-hero, Han Solo, is not allowed to remain one. He becomes a better man through the challenge to submit to authority and to sacrifice himself for others. Luke is repeatedly told by his master not to use evil means to defeat evil, because to do so is to become evil. He is warned against anger and the desire for vengeance and is exhorted to overcome them. In the concluding film, Luke chooses to abandon all powers, refusing to succumb to the temptation to use them in anger. It is this powerlessness that reveals his real moral strength, and this is the key component in the "conversion" of the evil Darth Vader. The final message of the series: Mercy and love are more powerful than sin and hate.

Even so, the film cannot be assessed as an isolated unit, as if it were hermetically sealed in an antiseptic isolation ward. It is a major cultural signpost, part of a larger culture shift. If *Dune* represents the new Gnosticism expressed aggressively and overtly, *Star Wars* represents a kind of "soft Gnosticism" in which the *gnosis* is an undercurrent beneath the surface waves of a few

Christian principles. It is important to recall at this point that during the second century there were several "Christian Gnostic" sects that attempted to reconcile Christianity and paganism and did so by incorporating many praiseworthy elements from the true faith. Similarly, Luke and company act according to an admirable moral code, but we must ask ourselves on what moral foundation this code is based, and what its source is. There is no mention of a transcendent God or any attempt to define the source of "the Force". And why is the use of psychic power considered acceptable? A major theme throughout the series is that good can be fostered by the use of these supernatural powers, which in our world are exclusively allied with evil forces. Moreover, the key figures in the overthrow of the malevolent empire are the Jedi masters, the enlightened élite, the initiates, the possessors of secret knowledge. Is this not Gnosticism?

At the very least these issues should suggest a close appraisal of the series by parents, especially since the films were revised and re-released in 1997, and a new generation of young people is being influenced by them. The most pressing question that should be asked is, which kind of distortion will do the more damage: blatant falsehood or falsehood mixed with the truths that we hunger for?

Vigilance, Paranoia, and Uncle Walt

No assessment of the situation should overlook the influence of Walt Disney Productions. Its unequalled accomplishments in the field of animation and in drama for children have made it a keystone in the culture of the West. Walt Disney became a kind of secular saint, a patron of childhood, the archangel of the young imagination. Some of this reputation was merited. Who among us has not been delighted and, indeed, formed by the films released in the early years of production, modern retellings of classic fairy stories such as *Sleeping Beauty, Pinocchio*, and *Snow White*. In these and other films, evil is portrayed as evil, and virtue as a moral struggle fraught with trial and error. Telling lies makes your nose grow long; indulging in vice turns you into a donkey; sorcery is a device of the enemy used against the good; witches are deadly. There are even moments that approach evangelization. In *Fantasia*, for example, "The Sorcerer's Apprentice" segment is a warning about dabbling in occult powers. In the final segment, "Night on Bald Mountain", the devil is shown in all his malice, seducing and raging, but defeated by the prayers of the saints. As the pilgrims process toward the dawn, they are accompanied by the strains of Schubert's "Ave Maria". Although there are parts of this film too frightening for small children, its final word is holiness.

Upon that reputation many parents learned to say, "Oh, it's by Disney. It must be okay!" But even in the early years of the Disney studios, the trends of modernity were present. As our culture continued to follow that tendency, films continued to diverge from the traditional Christian world view. *Snow White* and *Pinocchio* are perhaps the most pure interpretations of the original fairy tales, because the changes by Disney were of degree, not of kind. Much of the editing had to do with putting violence and other grotesque scenes off-screen (such as the demise of the wicked queen), because reading a story and seeing it are two different experiences, especially for children.

By the time *Cinderella* hit the theaters, the changes were more substantial. For example, Cinderella's stepsisters (in the Grimm version) were as beautiful as she, but vain and selfish. And the prince (in both the Grimm and Perrault versions) sees Cinderella in rags and ashes and still decides to love her, before she is transformed back into the beauty of the ball. These elements are changed in the Disney version, with the result that Cinderella wins the prince's hand, not primarily because of her virtue, but because she is the prettiest gal in town. Some prince!

Walt Disney died in 1966. During the late 1960s and 1970s the studio's approach gradually changed. Its fantasy and science fiction films began to show symptoms of the spreading moral confusion in that genre. "Bad guys" were at times presented as complex souls, inviting pity if not sympathy. "Good guys" were a little more tarnished than they once had been and, indeed, were frequently portrayed as foolish simpletons. A strain of "realism" had entered children's films—sadly so, because a child's hunger for literature (visual or printed) is his quest for a "more real world". He needs to know what is truly heroic in simple, memorable terms. He needs to see the hidden foundations of his world before the complexities and the nuances of the modern mind come flooding in to overwhelm his perceptions. The creators of the new classics had failed to grasp this timeless role of the fairy tale. Or, if they had grasped it, they arbitrarily decided it was time to change it. What began as a hairline crack began to grow into a chasm.

The Watcher in the Woods is a tale of beings from another dimension, séances, ESP, and channelling (spirits speaking through a human medium), a story that dramatically influences the young audience to believe that occult powers, though sometimes frightening, can bring great good for mankind. *Bedknobs and Broomsticks*, a comedy about a "good" witch, softens ancient fears about witchcraft. *Pete's Dragon* is the tale of a cute, friendly dragon who becomes a pal to the young hero and helps to defeat the "bad guys". In another time and place such films would probably be fairly harmless. Their impact must be understood in the context of the much larger movement that is inverting the symbol-life that grew from the Judeo-Christian revelation. This is more than just a haphazard development, more than just a gradual fading of right discernment in the wake of a declining Christian culture.

This is an anti-culture pouring in to take its place. Some of it is full-frontal attack, but much of it is subtler and pleasurably packaged. Still more of it seems apparently harmless. But the undermining of a child's perceptions in forms that are apparently harmless may be the most destructive of all.

By the 1990s, old fairy tales such as *Aladdin, Beauty and the Beast,* and *The Little Mermaid* were being remade by Walt Disney Productions in an effort to capture the imagination (and the market potential) of a new generation. *The Little Mermaid* represents an even greater break from the original intention of fairy stories than earlier retellings such as *Cinderella*. The mermaid's father is shown to be an unreasonable patriarchist and she justifiably rebellious. In order to obtain her desire (marriage to a land-based human prince), she swims away from home and makes a pact with an evil Sea Witch, who turns her into a human for three days, long enough to make the prince kiss her. If she can entice him to do so, she will remain a human forever and marry him. So far, the film is close to Hans Christian Andersen's original fairy story. But a radical departure is to be found in the way the plot resolves itself. Despite the disasters the little mermaid causes, only other people suffer the consequences of the wrong she has done, and in the end she gets everything she wants. Charming as she is, she is really a selfish brat whose only abiding impulse is a shallow romantic passion. In the original Andersen tale, the little mermaid faces some difficult moral decisions and decides for the good, choosing in the end to sacrifice her own desires so that the prince will remain happily married to his human bride. As a result of her self-denial, she is taken up into the sky among the "children of the air", the benign spirits who do good in the world.

"In three hundred years we shall float like this into the Kingdom of God!" one of them cries.

"But we may get there sooner!" whispers one of the daughters of the air. "Unseen, we fly into houses where there are children, and for every day that we find a good child who gives its parents joy . . . , God shortens the time of [our] probation."

Obviously there has been some heavy-handed editing in the film version, a trivialization of the characters, stripping the tale of moral content and references to God, with a net result that the meaning of the story is seriously distorted, even reversed. In a culture dominated by consumerism and pragmatism, it would seem that the best message modern producers are capable of is this: In the "real" world the "healthy ego" goes after what it wants. You can even play with evil and get away with it, maybe even be rewarded for your daring by hooking the handsomest guy in the land, winning for yourself your own palace, your own kingdom, and happiness on your own terms.

Harmless? I do not think so.

Aladdin especially represents the kind of films that are apparently harmless. To criticize it in the present climate is extremely difficult, because so many people in Christian circles have simply accepted it as "family entertainment". But *Aladdin* begs some closer examination.

The animated version is adapted from the *Arabian Nights*, a fairy tale that originated in Persia and reflects the beliefs of its Muslim author. According to the original tale, a magician hires a poor Chinese boy named Aladdin to go into an underground cave in search of a magic lamp that contains untold power. Aladdin is not merely poor, he is lazy. Through neglect of his duties, he failed to learn a trade from his father before he died and now is vulnerable to temptation. When he finds the lamp, Aladdin refuses to give it up and is locked in the cave. When he accidentally rubs the lamp a *jinn* (spirit) of the lamp materializes. In the Islamic religion the *jinni* are demonic spirits, intelligent, fiery beings of the air, who can take on many forms, including human and animal. Some *jinni* are better characters than others, but they are considered on the whole to be tricksters. According to Arabian mythology, they were created out of flame, while men and angels were created out of clay and light. Whoever controls a *jinn* is master of tremendous power, for the *jinn* is his slave. Aladdin, helped by such a spirit, marries the Sultan's daughter, and the *jinn* builds them a fabulous palace. But the wicked magician tricks them out of the lamp and transports the palace to Africa. Aladdin chases them there, regains the lamp in a heroic struggle, and restores the palace to China.

In the Disney remake, Aladdin is now a young hustler who speaks American urban slang in an Arabian marketplace. He is a likeable teenage thief who is poor through no fault of his own. He wants to make it big. When he meets the Sultan's daughter, who is fleeing the boring confinement of her palace, and rescues her through wit and "street-smarts", the romance begins. The film strives to remain true to some of the original plot, but in the characterization one sees evidence of the new consciousness. The film's genie is a comedian of epic proportions, changing his roles at lightning speed, so that the audience barely has time to laugh before the next sophisticated entertainment industry joke is trotted out. He becomes Ed Sullivan, the Marx Brothers, a dragon, a homosexual, female belly dancers, Pinocchio, and on and on. It is a brilliant and fascinating display. He is capable of colossal powers, and he is, wonder of wonders, Aladdin's slave. An intoxicating recipe for capturing a child's imagination.

This is a charming film. It contains some very fine scenes and deserves some praise for an attempt at morality. The genie, for example, admonishes the young master that there are limits to the wishes he can grant: no killing, no making someone fall in love with you, no bringing anyone back from the dead. Aladdin is really a "good thief", who robs from the comfortable and gives to the poor. He is called a "street-rat" by his enemies, yet he feels within himself aspirations to something better, something great. He is kind and generous to hungry, abandoned children; he defies the arrogant and the rich, and he is very, very brave. He is only waiting for an opportunity to show what sterling stuff he is made of. It is possible that this film may even have a good effect on the many urban children who live close to that level of poverty and desperation. By providing an attractive role model of a young person determined to overcome adversity, it may do much good in the world. There are even moments when spiritual insight is clear and true—when, for example, at the climax of the tale the magician takes on his true form, that of a gigantic serpent. And yet, there is something on the subliminal level, some undefinable warp in the presentation that leaves the discerning viewer uneasy.

Most obvious, perhaps, is the feeling of sensuality that dominates the plot. It is a romance, of course, and it must be understood that a large number of old literary fairy tales were also romances. But this is modern romance, complete with stirring music and visual impact. Aladdin and the Princess are both scantily clad throughout the entire performance, and, like so many characters in Disney animation, they appear to be bursting with hormones. There is a kiss that is more than a chaste peck. Nothing aggressively wrong, really. Nothing obscene, but all so thoroughly modern. At the very least, one should question the effect this stirring of the passions will have on the many children who flock to see the latest Disney cartoon. The cartoon, by its very nature, says "primarily for children". But this is, in fact, an adolescent romance, with some good old cartoon effects thrown in to keep the little ones' attention and some sly innuendo to keep the adults chuckling.

The handling of the supernatural element is, I believe, a more serious defect. To put it simply, the *jinn* is a demon. But such a charming demon. Funny and sad, clever and loyal (as long as you're his master), harmless, helpful, and endlessly entertaining.

Just the kind of guardian spirit a child might long for. Does this film implant a longing to conjure up such a spirit?

The film's key flaw is its presentation of the structure of reality. It is an utterly delightful advertisement for the concept of "the light side of the Force and the dark side of the Force", and as such it is a kind of cartoon *Star Wars*. Like Luke Skywalker, Aladdin is a young hero pitched against impossible odds, but the similarities do not end there. Luke becomes strong enough to battle his foes only by going down into a cave in a mysterious swamp and facing there "the dark side" of himself. Then, by developing supernatural powers, he is enabled to go forth to defeat the evil in the world. Similarly, Aladdin first seeks to obtain the lamp by going down into the jaws of a lionlike beast that rises up out of the desert and speaks with a ghastly, terrifying voice. The lamp of spiritual power resides in a cave in the belly the beast, and Aladdin *takes* it from him. Here is a clear message to the young who aspire to greater things: If you want to improve your lot in life, spiritual power is an even better possession than material powers such as wealth or physical force. It could be argued that Luke does not enlist the aid of demonic beings, nor does he cooperate with supernatural forces for selfish purposes. Indeed, he is a shining idealist. But this argument presumes that developing occult powers does not place one in contact with such evil beings—a very shaky presumption to say the least. At best there is an ambiguity in Luke's cooperation with "the Force" that leaves ample room for the young to absorb gnostic messages.

What is communicated about the nature of spiritual power in *Aladdin*? Leave aside for the moment the question of the hero being helped by a "good demon" to overcome a bad one. Leave aside also the problem of telling the young that they should ignore their natural terrors of the supernatural in order to succeed in their quests. Leave aside, moreover, the subtle inference that light and darkness, good and evil, are merely reverse sides of the same cosmic coin. There are subtler messages in the film. For example, a theme running throughout is that Aladdin is "worthy" to master such power, though we never learn what constitutes his worthiness. The viewer assumes that it is his bravado, cunning, and basically good heart. In reality, none of us is worthy of powers that properly belong to God alone. None of us is worthy of restoration to Paradise. Salvation is God's gift to mankind by the merits of his death on the Cross. Even so, we have not yet reached our one true home. We have all sinned and fallen short of the glory of God, and in this world no one is capable of wielding evil supernatural powers without being corrupted by them. It is modern man's ignorance of this principle that is now getting the world into a great deal of trouble. A powerful falsehood is implanted in the young by heroes who are given knowledge of good and evil, given power over good and evil, who play with evil but are never corrupted by it.

Beauty and the Beast handles the problem differently, but the end result is the same—the taming of the child's instinctive reaction to the image of the horrible. The Beast is portrayed as a devil-like being. He is not merely deformed or grotesque, as he is in the written fable. In the film his voice is unearthly and horrifying; he is sinister in appearance, his face a hideous mimicry of medieval gargoyles, his body a hybrid abomination of lion, bull, bear, and demon. His castle is full of diabolical statues. Of course, the central themes are as true and timeless as ever: Love sees beneath the surface appearance to the interior reality of the person; and love breaks the spell that evil casts over a life.

Yet here too there are disturbing messages: A "good witch" casts the spell in order to improve the Beast's character, implying that good ends come from evil means. But no truly good person does harm in order to bring about a good. While it is true that good can come out of evil situations, it is only because God's love is greater than evil. God's primary intention is that we always choose the good. In the original fairy tale, the spell is cast by an evil sorcerer, and the good conclusion to the plot is brought about in spite of him.

The Disney Beast really has a heart of gold. By contrast, handsome Gaston, the "normal" man, proves to be the real villain. He is a despicable parody of masculinity, a stupid, vain macho-man, who wishes to marry the heroine and chain her to the ennui of dull village life. The Beauty in the original tale embraces the virtues of hard work and the simple country life that result from

her father's misfortune. The Disney Beauty pines for something "better". There is a feminist message here, made even stronger by the absence of any positive male role models. Even her father is a buffoon, though loveable. This gross characterization of "patriarchy" would not be complete without a nasty swipe at the Church, and sure enough, Gaston has primed a clown-like priest to marry them. (The depiction of ministers of religion as either corrupt or ridiculous is practically unrelieved in contemporary films—Disney films are especially odious in this respect.)

To return for a moment to the question of beauty: A principle acknowledged in all cultures (except those in a terminal phase of self-destruction) is that physical beauty in creation is a living metaphor of spiritual beauty. The ideal always points to something higher than itself, to some ultimate good. In culture this principle is enfleshed, made visible. If at times spiritual beauty is present in unbeautiful fictional characters or situations, this only serves to underline the point that the physical is not an end in itself. In Disney's *Pocahontas* we find this principle inverted. Dazzling the viewer's eyes with superb scenes that are more like impressionistic paintings than solid narrative, stirring the emotions with haunting music and the supercharged atmosphere of sexual desire, its creators are really about a much bigger project than cranking out yet another tale of boy-meets-girl. Beauty is now harnessed to the task of promoting environmentalism and eco-spirituality. The real romance here is the mystique of pantheism, a portrayal of the earth as alive, animated with spirits (for example, a witchlike tree-spirit gives advice to Pocahontas about the nature of courtship). The earth and the flesh no longer point to something higher than themselves; they are ends in themselves. The "noble savage" understands this; the white, male, European Christian does not. And as usual, Disney portrays masculinity in its worst possible light (excepting only the hero, Smith, who is sensitive and confused). The other European males are rapacious predators, thoughtless builders, dominators, polluters, and killers; and those who are not any of the foregoing are complete nincompoops. It is all so predictable, all so very "consciousness-raising". What child does not take away from the film the impression that, in order to solve his problems, industrial-technological man need only reclaim the lost innocence of this pre-Columbian Eden?

I did not view Disney's *The Hunchback of Notre Dame* in a theater but watched the video release at home. The effect of the full-screen experience must have been overwhelming for audiences, because the visual effects in the video version were very impressive, clearly among Disney's most brilliant achievements in animation. However, I was disturbed by themes that have now become habitual with this studio. Within the first ten minutes of the story, a self-righteous Catholic moralist rides into the plot on horseback and chases a poor gypsy mother, who runs barefoot through the streets of Paris, carrying her baby in her arms, in a desperate attempt to reach the sanctuary of Notre Dame cathedral. She stumbles on the steps of the church and dies. The moralist picks up the baby, discovers that he is deformed, a "monster", and decides to dispose of him by dropping him down a well, all the while muttering pious imprecations against this "spawn of the devil". So far, not a great portrait of Catholicism. In the only redeeming moment in the film, a priest rushes out of the cathedral, sees the dead woman, and warns the moralist that his immortal soul is in danger. To amend for his sin, he must agree to be the legal guardian of the baby. The moralist agrees, on the condition that the monster be raised in secret in Notre Dame.

In the next scene the baby is now a young man, Quasimodo, a badly deformed hunchback who lives in isolation in the tower of the cathedral. He is the bell ringer, a sweet soul, humble, good, and creative, content to make art and little toys and to observe from his lonely height the life of the people of Paris. His solitude is broken only by the occasional visits of the moralist, who takes delight in reminding Quasimodo that he is a worthless monster who survives only because of his (the moralist's) "kindness". Is there anyone in the audience who has missed the point: The moralist is the ultimate hypocrite, the real monster. Quasimodo's only other friends are three gargoyles, charming, humorous little demons who are reminiscent of the Three Stooges. They encourage him to believe in love, to believe in himself, to have courage. In one interesting short scene, the gargoyles mock a carving of the Pope. Later in the film there is a scene depicting the churchgoers praying below in the cathedral. Without exception they pray for wealth, power, and gratification of their desires—a portrait of Catholics as utterly selfish, shallow people.

A sensual young gypsy woman flees into the cathedral to escape the moralist (who is also a judge). Safe inside, she prays for divine assistance in a vague, agnostic fashion. In stark contrast to the prayers of the Catholics, there is nothing selfish in her prayer. She merely asks for justice for her people. As the music swells, she turns away from the altar, still singing her "prayer", strolling in the opposite direction of the Catholics who are approaching the altar. Her supplication dissolves into a romantic musing that is more sentiment than insight into the nature of real mercy and justice. Disney's point is clear: Traditional Christianity is weak, blind, and selfish; "real Christianity" is sociological and "politically correct".

The romantic element, a mutual attraction between the gypsy woman and a young soldier, is simply a rehash of the screen romances that have become a necessary ingredient in Disney animated films. Lots of body language, lots of enticing flesh, a garish portrayal of the tormented moralist's secret lusts, a contrasting depiction of the beautiful young couple's sexual desire as pure and natural, and a sensual screen kiss that is inappropriate for young viewers (as it is in *Aladdin*, *The Little Mermaid*, and other Disney films). Perhaps we should ask ourselves if viewing such intimate moments between man and woman is ever appropriate, even for adults. Is voyeurism, in any form, good for the soul?

The Hunchback of Notre Dame concludes with a frenzied climax in which the forces of love and courage are pitted against the ignorance of the medieval Church. Quasimodo has overcome the lie of his worthlessness through the counsel of his gargoyles and is now strong enough to defy the moralist. He rescues the gypsy girl, who is about to be burned for witchcraft, and flees with her to the bell tower. There the moralist tracks them down (after first pushing aside the ineffectual priest who tries to stop him) and attempts to kill them. As one might expect, he comes to a bad end. The gypsy and the soldier are reunited, and Quasimodo makes do with platonic love. All's well that ends well.

Based on Victor Hugo's novel of the same title (published in 1831), the film retains much of the plot and characterization and even manages to communicate some truths. But the reality-shift evidenced in the modern version is a serious violation of the larger architecture of truth. The truths are mixed with untruths, and because of the sensory impact of the film medium, it is that much more difficult for an audience to discern rightly between the two. This is especially damaging to children, who because of their age are in a state of formation that is largely impressionistic. Moreover, most modern people do not know their history and do not possess the tools of real thought and thus are vulnerable to manipulation of their feelings. Young and old, we are becoming a race of impressionists.

Rather than thinking with ideas, we "think" in free-form layers of images loosely connected by emotions. There would be little harm in this if the sources of these images were honest. But few sources in culture and entertainment are completely honest these days. And even if the mind were well stocked with the best of images (a very rare state), it is still not equipped to meet the spiritual and ideological confusion of our times. The problem is much deeper than a lack of literacy, because even the mental imagery created by the printed word can be merely a chain of misleading impressions, however well articulated they may be. The real problem is *religious illiteracy*, by which I mean the lack of an objective standard against which we can measure our subjective readings of sensation and experience. Without this objective standard, one's personal gnosis will inevitably push aside the objective truth and subordinate it to a lesser position, when it does not banish it altogether. That is why a modern maker of culture who feels strongly that Catholicism is bad for people has no qualms about rewriting history or creating anti-Catholic propaganda and will use all the powers of the modern media to do so.

One wonders what Disney studios would do with Hugo's *Les Miserables* (published in 1862), an expressly Christian story in which two central characters, the bishop and Jean Valjean, are heroic Catholics fighting for truth, mercy, and justice in the face of the icy malice of the secular humanists, against the background of the French Revolution. Would the scriptwriters and executives sanitize and politically correct these characters by de-Catholicizing them? It would be interesting to observe the contortions necessary for such a transformation. Perhaps they would do what Hollywood did to Dominique Lapierre's wonderful book, *The City of Joy*. The central character in that true story, a Christlike young priest who chose to live among the most abject of Calcutta's poor, is entirely replaced in the film version by a handsome young American doctor (who was a secondary character in the book). In the Hollywood rewrite, the doctor is idealistic but amoral, and he is in the throes of an identity crisis. Uncertain at first if he is merely a technician of the body, slowly awakening to the possibility that he might become a minister to the whole person, in the end he chooses the latter. Following the gnostic pattern, he becomes the *knower* as healer, the scientist as priest. It is a well-made film, containing some good insights and moving scenes, but by displacing the priest of Christ, it loses an important part of the original story's "soul", cheating us of the real meaning of the events on which it is based.

Where Catholicism is not simply weeded out of the culture, it is usually attacked, though the attacks tend to be swift cheapshots. Take, for instance, Steven Spielberg's smash hit, *Jurassic Park*.

Again, there is much to recommend this film, such as the questions it raises about science and morality, especially the issue of genetic engineering. In the struggle between people and dinosaurs there is plenty of human heroism, and the dinosaurs are even presented as classic reptiles—no taming or befriending here. So far so good. On the level of symbolism, however, we are stunned with an image of the reptile as practically omnipotent. The *Tyrannosaurus rex* is power incarnate, and its smaller cousin, the *Velociraptor,* is not only fiercely powerful, it is intelligent and capable of learning.

There is a telling scene in which the most despicable character in the film, a sleazy lawyer, is riding in a car with two young children. When a dinosaur approaches the car to destroy it, the lawyer abandons the children to their fate and flees into an outdoor toilet cubicle. The T-Rex blows away the flimsy structure, exposing the lawyer, who is seated on the "john", quivering uncontrollably and whining the words of the Hail Mary. The T-Rex picks him up in its jaws, crunches hard, and gulps him down its throat. In the theater where I saw the film, the audience cheered.

Where Is It All Leading?

At this point, the reader may be saying to himself, "What you describe may be true. I've seen evidence of it, and I've struggled to understand it. I've tried to pick my way through the flood of things coming at my children, but I'm not having much success. I'm uneasy about the new culture, but I don't seem to have the skills to argue with it."

I think most conscientious parents feel this way. We know something is not right, but we don't quite know how to assess it. We worry that our children might be affected adversely by it, but at the same time we don't want to overreact. The image of the "witch-hunt" haunts us (a fear that is strongly reinforced by the new culture), but we are equally concerned about the need to protect our children from being indoctrinated into paganism. What, then, are we to do?

Our first step must be in the direction of finding a few helpful categories, a standard against which we can measure examples of the new culture. I have found it useful to divide the field of children's culture into roughly four main categories:

1. Material that is entirely good.
2. Material that is fundamentally good but disordered in some details.
3. Material that appears good on the surface but is *fundamentally* disordered.
4. Material that is blatantly evil, rotten to the core.

I will return to these categories in the next chapter's assessment of children's literature, where I hope to develop them in greater detail. I introduce them here to make a different point. Two generations ago the culture of the Western world was composed of material that, with few exceptions, was either entirely good (1) or fundamentally good but disordered in some details (2). About forty years ago there began a culture-shift that steadily gathered momentum, a massive influx of material that appeared good on the surface but was fundamentally disordered (3). It became the new majority. During this period entirely good material became the minority, and at the same time more material that was diabolically evil began to appear (4). There is a pattern here. And it raises the question: Where is it all leading?

I think it highly unlikely that we will ever see a popular culture that is wholly dominated by the blatantly diabolical, but I do believe that unless we recognize what is happening, we may soon be living in a culture that is totally dominated by the fundamentally disordered and in which the diabolical is respected as an alternative world view and becomes more influential than the entirely good. Indeed, we may be very close to that condition. I can think of half a dozen recent films that deliberately reverse the meaning of Christian symbols and elevate the diabolical to the status of a saving mythology.

The 1996 film *DragonHeart*, for example, is the tale of a tenth-century kingdom that suffers under a tyrannical king. When the king is killed in a peasant uprising, his son inherits the crown but is himself wounded when he is accidentally impaled on a spike. His heart is pierced, and he is beyond all hope of recovery. The queen takes her son into an underground cave that is the lair of a dragon. She kneels before the dragon, calls him "Lord", and begs him to save the prince's life. The dragon removes half of his own heart and inserts it into the gaping wound of the prince's chest, then heals the wound with a touch of his claw.

The queen says to her son, "He [the dragon] will save you." And to the dragon she says, "He [the prince] will grow in your grace." The prince recovers and grows to manhood, the dragon's heart beating within him.

The prince becomes totally evil, a tyrant like his father, and the viewer is led to believe that, in this detail at least, traditional symbolism is at work—the heart of a dragon will make a man into a dragon. Not so, for later we learn that the prince's own evil nature has overshadowed the dragon's good heart. When the dragon reappears in the plot and becomes the central character, we begin to learn that he is not the terrifying monster we think him to be. He dabbles in the role the superstitious peasants have assigned to him (the traditional concept of dragon), but he never really does any harm, except to dragon slayers, and then only when they attack him without provocation. Through his growing friendship with a reformed dragon slayer, we gradually come to see the dragon's true character. He is wise, noble, ethical, and witty. He merely plays upon the irrational fears of the humans regarding dragons because he knows that they are not yet ready to understand the higher wisdom, a vision known only to dragons and their enlightened human initiates. It is corrupt human nature, we are told, that has deformed man's understanding of dragons.

The dragon and his knight-friend assist the peasants in an uprising against the evil prince. Even a Catholic priest is enlisted in the battle. This character is yet another Hollywood buffoon-priest, who in his best moments is a silly, poetic dreamer and at worst a confused and shallow remnant of a dishonored Christian myth. Over and over again, we are shown the ineffectiveness of Christianity against evil and the effective power of The People when they ally themselves with the dragon. The priest sees the choice, abandons his cross, and takes up a bow and arrow, firing two shafts into the head and groin of a practice dummy. In a final battle, he overcomes his Christian scruples and begins to shoot at enemy soldiers, quoting Scripture humorously (even the words of Jesus) every time he shoots. An arrow in a soldier's buttock elicits the priest's sly comment, "Turn the other cheek, brother!" When he aims at the evil prince, he murmurs, "Thou shalt not kill! Thou shalt not kill!" then proceeds to disobey the divine commandment. The arrow goes straight into the prince's heart, but he does not fall. He pulls the arrow from his heart and smiles. Neither Christian myth nor Christian might can stop this kind of evil!

Here we begin to understand the objectives that the script-writer has subtly hatched from the very beginning of the film. The prince cannot die because a dragon's heart beats within him, even though he, not the dragon, has corrupted that heart. The evil prince will die only when the dragon dies. Knowing this, the dragon willingly sacrifices his own life in order to end the reign of evil, receiving a spear thrust into his heart. At this point we see the real purpose of the film—the presentation of the dragon as a Christ-figure!

Shortly before this decisive climax, the dragon describes in mystical tones his version of the history of the universe: "Long ago, when man was young and the dragon already old, the wisest of our race took pity on man. He gathered together all the dragons, who vowed to watch over man always. And at the moment of his death, the night became alive with those stars [pointing to the constellation Draco], and thus was born the dragon's heaven."

He explains that he had shared his heart with the dying young prince in order to "reunite man and dragon and to ensure my place among my ancient brothers of the sky".

In the final moments of the film, after the dragon's death, he is assumed into the heavens amidst heart-throbbing music and star bursts and becomes part of the constellation Draco. The crowd of humans watch the spectacle, their faces filled with religious awe. A voice-over narrator says that in the years following "Draco's sacrifice" a time of justice and brotherhood came upon the world, "golden years warmed by an unworldly light. And when things became most difficult, Draco's star shone more brightly for all of us who knew where to look."

Few members of the audience would know that, according to the lore of witchcraft and Satanism, the constellation Draco is the original home of Satan and is reverenced in their rituals. Here is a warning about where Gnosticism can lead. What begins as one's insistence on the right to decide the meaning of good and evil leads inevitably to spiritual blindness. Step by step we are led from the wholly good to flawed personal interpretations of good; then, as the will is weakened and the mind darkened, we suffer more serious damage to the foundation itself and arrive finally, if we should lose all reason, at some manifestation of the diabolical.

When this process is promulgated with the genius of modern cinematic technology, packaged in the trappings of art and mysticism, our peril increases exponentially. My wife and I have known devout, intelligent, Christian parents who allowed their young children to watch *DragonHeart* because they thought it was "just mythology". This is an understandable naïveté, but it is also a symptom of our state of unpreparedness. The evil in corrupt mythology is never rendered harmless simply because it is encapsulated in a literary genre, as if sealed in a watertight compartment. Indeed, there are few things as infectious as mythology.

We would be sadly mistaken if we assumed that the cultural invasion is mainly a conflict of abstract ideas. It is a major front in the battle for the soul of modern man, and as such it necessarily entails elements of spiritual combat. For this reason parents must ask God for the gifts of wisdom, discernment, and vigilance during these times. We must also plead for extraordinary graces and intercede continuously for our children. The invasion reaches into very young minds, relaxing children's instinctive aversion to what is truly frightening. It begins there, but we must understand that it will not end there, for its logical end is a culture that exalts the diabolical. There are a growing number of signs that this process is well under way.

In most toy shops, for example, one can find a number of soft, cuddly dragons and other monsters to befriend. There are several new children's books about lovable dragons who are not evil, merely misunderstood. In one such book, given as a Christmas present to our children by a well-meaning friend, we found six illustrations that attempted to tame the diabolical by dressing it in ingratiating costumes. The illustrator exercised a certain genius that made his work well nigh irresistible. One of the images portrayed a horrible, grotesque being at the foot of a child's bed. The accompanying story told how the child, instead of driving it away, befriended it, and together they lived happily ever after. The demonic being had become the child's guardian. One wonders what has become of guardian angels! Such works seek to help children integrate "the dark side" into their natures, to reconcile good and evil within, and, as our friend expressed it, to "embrace their shadows".

In *Lilith*, a classical fantasy by the nineteenth-century Christian writer George MacDonald, the voice of Eve calls this darkness "the mortal foe of my children". In one passage a character describes the coming of "the Shadow":

> He was nothing but blackness. We were frightened the moment we saw him, but we did not run away, we stood and watched him. He came on us as if he would run over us. But before he reached us he began to spread and spread, and grew bigger and bigger, till at last he was so big that he went out of our sight, and we saw him no more, and then he was upon us.

It is when they can no longer see him that his power over them is at its height. They then describe how the shadow temporarily possessed them and bent their personalities in the direction of hatred. He is thrown off by love welling up within their hearts.

The German writer Goethe, in his great classic work *Faust*, uses a different approach to depict the seduction of mankind. At one point the devil says:

> Humanity's most lofty power,
> Reason and knowledge pray despise!
> But let the Spirit of all lies
> With works of dazzling magic blind you,
> Then absolutely mine, I'll have and bind you!

In children's culture a growing fascination with the supernatural is hastening the breakdown of the Christian vision of the spiritual world and the moral order of the universe. Reason and a holy knowledge are despised, while intoxicating signs and wonders increase.

Chapter V

Neopagan Literature for Children

Educators are rightly concerned that young people are not learning to enjoy reading. But in an effort to stimulate interest, they are introducing many books of questionable merit. Few things are as stimulating to the young as the mysterious and forbidden, and teachers know this. As a result, neopagan literature is making its way into classroom reading programs, public and private school libraries, and the children's section of public libraries.[1] As the appetite for fantasy increases, the industry grows, and writers and publishers turn to it in droves. Of course, some fantasy titles are of good quality, written in the Christian tradition of George MacDonald, J. R. R. Tolkien, and C. S. Lewis. Others are blatantly anti-Christian—easy enough to identify. But in the wide zone between the two poles there is a large and growing body of children's literature that is actually spiritual indoctrination wrapped in pleasing adventure packages. This kind of fiction may be the most harmful of all; it is also the most difficult to identify.

Why Has the West Become Neopagan?

Neopaganism, although it holds some beliefs in common with the old paganism, is very different from the classical paganism of Greece and Rome and the cultic paganism of the more bloodthirsty ancient religions. It is essentially a slide back *into* the

---

[1] I use the term "neopagan" in its proper definition: revived paganism or new paganism, not half-pagan or semi-pagan, which is how it is sometimes (incorrectly) used.

darkness of pre-Christianity, and that is a much graver spiritual problem than the condition of those peoples who were groping their way *out* of the darkness. The latter were ignorant, cruel, and in spiritual bondage, because they had not yet encountered the light of the one true God. The modern neopagan has known that light yet chooses to explore the darkness again. Regardless of what he might think about his position on the spiritual map, he is in no way standing upon firm land. Neopaganism is not a permanent state: it is neither fully pagan nor fully Christian. It is a transition. It is a downward slide.

Why is this happening? And how is it happening? The answer to these compelling questions is complex and would demand a lengthy examination of the history of the Western world, a separate study that is beyond the purposes of this book.[2] But perhaps at this point we need only consider a rough sketch of the processes that have led to our current confusion. The modernity of our times is the result of a series of historical developments in man's understanding of human nature, God, and the universe. Christian Humanism, which began as a reflection on the nature of man and his place in the cosmos, gradually mutated over the centuries, influenced by many social, political, philosophical, and religious factors. The Protestant Reformation, for example, elevated the authority of Sacred Scripture but at the same time instituted the principle of the individual's right to interpret that Scripture as he saw fit, thus placing man *above* the Word. Human subjectivity became a kind of autonomous magisterial authority cut off from the combined charisms of the universal Church, resulting in the proliferation of tens of thousands of Protestant sects, each with its own interpretation.

Secular humanism arose from the seedbed of a fragmented

[2] Readers interested in these questions should obtain a copy of the highly readable, insightful book, *What Is Secular Humanism?* by James Hitchcock (Ann Arbor, Mich.: Servant Books, 1982).

Christianity, which the new agnostics believed to be thoroughly discredited by its internal contradictions and religious wars. During the so-called "Enlightenment" of the eighteenth century, the rise of science, the outbreak of revolutions, and the emergence of the modern political state all worked toward devaluing man's sense of the hierarchical creation, turning his attention and energies to the immanent world, where he sought to build the City of Man—his dream of a secular salvation.

In the following century a branch of humanism developed that attempted to make a final break with the concept of God and religion. James Hitchcock describes it as follows:

> The strain of modern Humanism which comes down through Feuerbach, Marx, and Nietzsche can be called Promethean Humanism, after the figure in Greek mythology who stole fire from the gods and gave it to man. It is a Humanism that bases itself on rebellion and a denial of God. . . . The new Humanism of the nineteenth century embodied a demonic urge to negate and destroy. As Nietzsche saw clearly, it was not only a matter of not believing in God. Once God had been denied, man could achieve true freedom only by denying all moral constraints on himself and inventing his own morality. The human will alone became sovereign.[3]

Obviously, a society based on demonic urges will not survive very long. But negation and destruction can take less horrible forms than Nazism or Stalinism. Societies that reject the absolute moral law based on divine authority while maintaining a more or less benign veneer for a time may in the long run bring about a more thorough destruction of man, because they do not at first reveal themselves for what they are. We must keep in mind that the key concept of modern humanism is the sovereign

[3] Ibid., p. 48.

human will. But what can this possibly mean in terms of nation states and entire peoples? Does some mystical sovereign will of "the people" exist? No, it does not, because a population composed of autonomous individuals, each armed with his "sovereign will", is a recipe for total chaos. For this reason, authority in a secularized "democratic cosmos" has become more and more concentrated in the hands of a new class of social engineers, the group C. S. Lewis called the Conditioners. The power of man to make of himself what he pleases, Lewis pointed out, actually means the power of some men to make other men into what they please.[4]

On every level of modern society the Conditioners shape and reshape our concepts of reality, and these concepts are overwhelmingly secular humanist. Education, communications media, high culture, low culture, political theory, psychology, and so on, have all been affected to their very roots; even Christian theology and Scripture scholarship have been infected by so-called "demythologizing", which would reduce salvation history to the politics of Flatland, in which only a social salvation is desirable or possible. Our century, the age of genocide and total war, is also the age of utopian dreams.

But man is more than a social animal. He is an immortal soul, regardless of whether he denies or accepts this truth about himself, and thus he cannot live long without a spirituality of some kind. In the spiritual vacuum created by secular humanism, he has begun to cast about in every direction, searching for a set of concepts that might reconnect him to a much larger universe, might reassure him that he is more than just a clever talking beast. He is especially drawn to those concepts that do not demand of him any moral constraints, for outside restrictions on his desires would be a threat to his sovereign self.

---

[4] *The Abolition of Man* (New York: Collier Books, Macmillan Publishing, 1955), p. 72.

The Gnostic streams that had bubbled below the surface of Western society for many centuries, erupted during the nineteenth century in occult movements and new religions, then swelled into a flood tide during the latter half of this century. We would be mistaken if we were to think of this phenomenon as a purely psychological, philosophical, or sociological development. There is a spiritual element involved here also, one that has manifested itself powerfully and perhaps in unprecedented ways. There is much evidence of the influence of evil spirits, and they are especially active in those circles that encourage spirituality that is not in submission to the law of God. To put it simply, we now find ourselves in a war zone. But the nature of this war, though relentless and increasing in intensity, is not so much open combat as it is guerrilla warfare. We should not assume that, just because a few fright shows such as *The Exorcist* or Stephen King novels testify to the reality of supernatural evil, modern man will awake to his danger and seek real help. Such entertainments simply treat the devil as some kind of cosmic bogeyman, mythologizing him, rendering him so grotesque that he becomes unthinkably distant and unreal—sealed in a horror flick. In fact, Satan *is* truly horrible, but he wins people over by presenting sin and error and dangerous spiritual activities as something attractive. And no spirituality is more attractive to the sovereign self than neopaganism.

Madeleine L'Engle's "Christian" Neopaganism

A case in point is Madeleine L'Engle's fantasy series for young adults. Without reading these novels, I had invested implicit trust in them because I had heard that the author is a Christian writer of considerable talent. Furthermore, the first novel of the series had won the Newbery Award and is now being used in many elementary schools. Before allowing our children access to them, however, I paused and listened to a faint inner warning bell. I decided to read the books myself. At first glance I was delighted to find strong elements of a supernatural faith. In the opening novel, *A Wrinkle in Time*, the reader is presented with a vast struggle between the powers of good and evil. Elements of the battle are portrayed accurately and with some insight into the devices of the evil spirits. So far so good. Like many a parent I heaved a sigh of relief that such a good writer had chosen to state her loyalty to the Judeo-Christian world view. As I read on, however, it became apparent that the author had woven into these gripping tales some elements about which one should have second thoughts.

First of all, the world of the L'Engle novels is our own; her heroes and heroines are the kids down the block. They are highly attractive role models. And in our world the kinds of things they are involved in actually spell spiritual disaster. The three central characters, Meg Murray, Charles Wallace Murray, and Calvin O'Keefe, are children with unusual psychic powers. They are guided in their fight against the forces of darkness by three "angels". One of the angels, curiously, has no scruples about stealing, and another materializes as a witch. That is not its true form, the angel assures the children, it is merely playing. Nevertheless, it is an odd image for an angel to use, considering the fact that in the real order of the cosmos witchcraft is involved with, or at least opens doors to, the world of the diabolical. Clearly the author is venting a popular modern notion about Christendom's horror of witchcraft. She is trying to tame the image of the witch and to show us that certain Christian fears about the supernatural are groundless— an undercurrent throughout her books. In another novel she portrays Christians condemning to death (for witchcraft) a woman who is involved in herbalism and extrasensory perception.

A central theme in L'Engle's novels is that people endowed with extrasensory perception are the vanguard of civilization and the guardians of mankind. Interestingly, the three children who are gifted in this way are not particularly virtuous; they are, rather, chosen to save the world because of their great intellects and their psychic powers. Throughout her books there are a number of references to God, but regarding Jesus we learn only that he was a "great fighter" for the good, alongside Buddha, Shakespeare, and Einstein. To further the children's understanding, the angels conduct them to the "Happy Medium"—an occult medium who gives them clairvoyant vision. The knowledge they obtain assists them in their quest. There are many such odd inversions of reality in the series. For example, one of the least attractive characters is Calvin's mother. Mrs. O'Keefe is a toothless, bad-tempered hag, ground down by fate and the mothering of eleven children. In a later novel we are told that she too is spiritually gifted with a mixture of Irish-Christian and pagan-Celtic myth, but this has been buried under the burdens of raising a large family.

In *A Swiftly Tilting Planet,* L'Engle again examines the struggle between good and evil on the spiritual and the historical plane. The hero, Charles Wallace, travels through time to various eras and enters "within" the personalities of several characters in order to redirect their thoughts and their choices, thereby altering history in the direction of good. By inhabiting his "hosts", he makes it possible for the world to avoid a looming nuclear war. The plot line and theology are very clever, always entertaining, and at times moving. However, the author ignores some crucial Christian wisdom about the supernatural.

It is never permissible (even if it were possible) to "inhabit" or possess the body, mind, or any level of another's being. That would be a violation of the fundamental law of freedom that God has written into human nature. It is the devil who attempts to possess people. Of course, the horrible nature of diabolical possession makes it obviously repugnant. L'Engle attempts to make a case for benevolent possession—all for a good purpose, of course, and with nothing repugnant to make us nervous. But there is a lie at work here: one that says that we can achieve good by some kind of sanitized version of supernatural powers. One that says, "Well, yes, these powers have been the domain of evil for a long time—far too long—so let us reclaim them, make them our own." This attitude ignores completely the warning found in Genesis, where we observe the devil's first and most productive temptation to man: to be like gods. It rejects the truth that in man's fallen condition such powers will always tend to evil because they feed our root sin, which is pride. Supernatural power belongs to God alone; only he and his holy angels are capable of exercising it for good ends.

There are other questionable themes throughout the novel, chief of which is the idea that there is ultimately no difference between pagan and Christian spiritualities. The only characters who contradict this idea are representatives of organized religion, notably a vicious, despicable minister of a Puritan church. By contrast, the most sensitive, loving, visionary characters in the novels have a fondness for chants and crystal-ball gazing. The chants are sometimes Christian, sometimes pagan, and the line between the two is curiously blurred.

In *A Wind at the Door* the author continues to soften and bend traditional Christian symbols. When a cherub appears to Charles, the latter mistakes it for a dragon. A pet snake named Louise is a wise creature capable of communicating with the three young heroes by "kything", an advanced form of mental telepathy. In fact, just about every creature, ranging from a microscopic organism to a nine-foot-high cosmic "Teacher", is capable of this art, including the three young humans. Thus equipped, Charles, Meg, and Calvin set forth to save the universe from the attacks of the Echthroi, which are evil spirits. The cherub informs the children that "your mythology would call them fallen angels."

The major theme of the story is that things have being when they are named. The Echthroi attempt to keep us from finding our true identity, and they seek to un-name all things, thereby destroying creation itself. In a final battle, Meg cries out, "Echthroi! You are Named! My arms surround you. You are no longer nothing. You are. You are filled. You are me. You are Meg." Instantly, the battle is won, and the universe is on the way to restoration.

A very interesting theology is dramatized in this climax. The author appears to believe that if evil spirits are embraced, they will cease to have power; they will be absorbed into oneself or filled with oneself (implying that evil is merely an absence of good, a vacuum, a nonbeing or unbeing). While it is true in one sense that evil is the absence of good, that is not the whole truth, for in reality the evil spirits are more than an absence of light. They are conscious, willfully distorted beings. They are absolutely corrupt angelic persons. To think that one might pacify them is similar to thinking one can tame a hungry shark or an angry scorpion if one loves it enough. This sentimentality (and it is not so rare as we might suppose) is really based on a misunderstanding of the nature of various beings. Modern psychology has played its part in the decline of discernment of spirits: If we are to believe that there are no longer any evil persons (in the sense of people completely ruled by evil), and if such people are now to be considered merely ill, does it not follow that there are now no longer such things as evil spirits, merely sick ones? In the end, does the salvation of the world come down to finding an appropriate cosmic therapy?

The great father of Western theology, Saint Thomas Aquinas, would not agree. He teaches that when the fallen angels made their decision to rebel against God, they made an eternal choice, and their natures were radically altered forever. They became a different kind of being than they had been. For eternity they will not depart from that nature, just as the good angels remain ever true to their essential nature, just as the baby bunny, the scorpion, the lamb, and the tiger are true to their essential natures. It is only human beings who remain in a state of uncertainty. We have been damaged in our essential nature, and we are being restored to our true image and likeness by the action of grace, through Christ's redemption. Yet until we reach Paradise, we will continue to be pulled this way and that in a great cosmic tug of war. The mind of man is a major battlefront, and an important part of the struggle takes place in literature. Our truest stories tell us who we are and where we should be going. They inform us about the nature of the enemy. They strengthen us for the journey. A badly flawed tale, on the other hand, can weaken and confuse us. It may direct us into some very dangerous territory.

That is why we need to exercise discernment in children's literature, a discernment that is not always easy, especially when the author writes with a certain flourish that is both thought-provoking and very entertaining. Certain questions should be asked by parents who are considering using books such as L'Engle's fantasy series in their family: What is the long-term influence of literary characters who not only lack spiritual discernment about the enticements of the enemy but also actually embrace those enticements as their natural birthright, as forces for good? If our children identify with these lovable, engaging heroes and heroines, can this undermine the soul's natural defenses? And what are the long-term effects of portraying as hidebound bigots anyone who opposes a synthesis of Christianity and those pagan practices that are forbidden by God and his Church?

Granted, parents might find in these books an opportunity to deepen their children's understanding. Perhaps this might work for some exceptionally mature children of solid faith. The story could be read for pleasure, and then a parent might ask the children important questions: Did they spot the confused ideas, the untruths, the popular modern myths? Even so, parents should consider carefully and pray much before doing so, because they are definitely taking a risk. Thereafter they will have to debate against the subconscious power of several novels packed with potent images that have been lodged deeply in the child's mind. And in a child's mind an image often has greater authority than the voice of a parent droning on and on about seemingly abstract dangers. Those dangers are quite real, but they are invisible, and the eye of childhood is highly sensual.

We are living in confused times, and it is not surprising that gifted creators—yes, even Christian creators—sometimes get their ideas tilted and their spiritual perceptions wrinkled. One cannot help but wonder about the author's intentions. It is true that L'Engle depicts very well the malice of evil spirits, and does so at a time when many modern people have lost the sense of spiritual warfare. So many are pursuing supernatural contacts and experiences as if the need for a spiritual life were just one more appetite to be filled. Did she wish to reach the growing number of children raised in such families? If so, it is possible that these novels might provide a stepping stone for drifting souls to find their way back to Christianity. But I think this a very small possibility. Stepping stones go in both directions, and it is far more likely that in the minds of good but naïve Christian families the ground is being prepared to accept a spiritually disastrous philosophy.

There is no perfect work of art, nor is there any work of fiction that does not in some small or large way fall short of a complete vision of reality. But there is a crucial difference between a flawed detail and a flaw in the fundamental vision. A house with a weak window frame is not nearly so dangerous as a house built on sand. Madeleine L'Engle's fantasy tales have got many details right, but the foundation is wrong.

In a fallen world it is necessary to "test the spirits", to discern many things, to look beneath surface appearances and to see beyond delightful styles to the essence of what is being communicated. The sense of truth is not easily come by without prayer, long labor, and experience. If we choose to allow works such as L'Engle's fantasy tales to form our children's minds, we should do so with great caution. On the whole, I think it unwise. My wife and I have decided to refrain from introducing the series to our children, and from now on we will consider with wariness any books in that genre of children's fiction.

The task remains: How are we to instill in our children a true vision of the shape of reality? There is a wealth of superb literature for the young, and it would take more than a lifetime of reading to exhaust it. The question is, how are we to find it, and if we find it, how are we to recognize it? How are Christian parents to pick their way through a minefield of confusing signs? A simple rule of thumb is to ask the following questions when assessing a book, video, or film: Does the story reinforce my child's understanding of the moral order of the universe? Or does it undermine it? Does it do some of both? Do I want that? What precisely is the author saying about the nature of evil? What does he tell the reader (or viewer) about the nature of the war between good and evil?

The Gray Zone

At this point I would like to return briefly to our makeshift scale of values for children's culture [see page 86]. Although I have divided the scale roughly into four general categories, there are, of course, many possible subcategories. The most obvious categories, 1 and 4, pertain to material that is wholly good or blatantly evil. Thoughtful parents will readily discern between these two opposites. However, in my correspondence and discussions with parents, one of the recurring questions that arises is: How do we discern between category 2, material that is fundamentally good but disordered in some details, and category 3, material that appears good on the surface but is fundamentally disordered?

A large number of titles are to be found in this wide gray zone, and it is impossible for most parents to examine more than a handful of them. But perhaps a few examples may be helpful at this point: Stephen Lawhead, Lloyd Alexander, Terry Brooks, Anne McCaffrey, and Ursula Le Guin are five of the most popular writers of fantasy fiction for young adults. Their books sell in the millions and can be found in most public libraries and many school libraries. These authors offer exciting plots, vivid characterization, and varying degrees of moral content. Each depicts a battle between good and evil. Of the five, Lawhead and Alexander present a vision that is closest to the Judeo-Christian moral universe, though with some serious flaws.

Stephen Lawhead is an avowed Christian and not infrequently incorporates godly ideas into his tales. In *Dream Thief* there are strong Christian notes, even a short section that presents a band of Christian survivors as heroes. His major works are *The Dragon King Trilogy* (an epic struggle between the followers of the "Most High" and devotees of the "old gods") and *The Pendragon Cycle* (his series on the Arthurian legend). Both contain good insights about the spiritual quest. However, parents should preview these novels to determine if the author's use of symbols is always prudent. There is sometimes a subtle drift toward a blending of pagan and Christian spirituality, though it is nowhere near as blatant as it is in many comparable works by other authors. With Lawhead, it is the undercurrents, the implications, the blurring, that leave one uneasy. Parents should note, also, that in some of Lawhead's books fornication is part of the plot, though the author does not glamorize it. If pressed to locate Lawhead on our scale,

I would say that some of his books are in category 2 (material that is fundamentally good but disordered in some details); other Lawhead titles are closer to category 3 (material that appears good on the surface but is fundamentally disordered).

Similarly, Lloyd Alexander's novels are a mixed bag. In *Westmark* the young hero, Theo, questions whether the end can ever justify the means. Alexander's *Prydain Chronicles* are his best known works, very popular with young adult readers. The five volumes in the series are primarily about the coming of age of a young pig keeper named Taran. This engaging lad is the servant of a wizard and caretaker of an oracle-pig. He plays a central role in the struggle against a sinister warlord, the Horned King, and a host of evil warriors, the Cauldron-Born, who are dead bodies brought back to life by bad magic for the purposes of serving the Horned King's evil designs. As in so many fantasy novels, "good" magic is allied with genuine virtues for the purpose of defeating evil. In comparison to Lawhead's novels, I would locate Alexander's farther down the scale toward category 3 (appears good but is fundamentally disordered). But the problem with both authors is an ambiguity regarding what is "good magic" and "bad magic". It could be argued that their approach is perfectly acceptable because, like Tolkien and Lewis, they are involved in "sub-creation". But there is an important difference: the neopagan sub-creation is very unlike Tolkien's or Lewis', for they portrayed original worlds in which the use of magic and clairvoyance is revealed as fraught with extreme danger. They demonstrate clearly the hidden seduction in the very powers that the neopagan proposes as instruments for the salvation of mankind.

Having said this, I think it important to underline the point that there is no scientific method for precisely measuring the spiritual value of novels in the gray zone. I believe that beyond the few basic guidelines discussed in this book, a parent's primary tool for discernment must be his own interior barometer. We all need to develop this faculty. We must pray for a spirit of vigilance and for a spirit of discernment, asking the Holy Spirit to prompt us whenever we try to assess a given author or title.

Terry Brooks, Anne McCaffrey, and Ursula Le Guin sometimes write within the boundaries of the gray zone, but they are definitely farther along the spectrum toward the pagan world view than Lawhead and Alexander. Some of their novels are clearly in category 3, with a drift in the direction of category 4. In Brooks' *First King of Shannara*, for example, the Druids are depicted as good guys who study the arcane knowledge of "good magic" in order to defeat the bad guys, deformed Druids who have fallen prey to the darker seductions of the magic arts. There is no clear explanation of what would prevent an individual involved in cultic magic from sliding inexorably into the dark side of such powers. It bears repeating here that in the real world there is no "light side" to occult activity; all such involvement, even so-called "good magic" or "white magic", is an exposure to the influence of the fallen angels, to the primeval serpent, the dragon that is known as Satan. In another Brooks novel, *The Tangle Box*, a dragon assists in the defeat of demons and gives the hero a ride on its back in exchange for a box of magic power, which the dragon promises never to open. The author explains that the dragon will keep his word: "He extended his firm and unbreakable promise. He gave his dragon's oath . . . a dragon's word was his bond." Why do I not feel reassured? Brooks' most recent novel, *Running with the Demon*, published in 1997, is a feverish horror tale of magic, demons, and monsters. The moral structure of this universe is totally scrambled: The author pits two forces against each other, "the Void" (representing evil) and "the Word" (representing good), but some of the servants of the Word are hideous and malicious; the Void is completely evil, and the Word is a mixture of good and evil. This novel is an example of where the gray zone can lead the young reader. I would categorize it as a definite 4—rotten to the core.

In Anne McCaffrey's enormously popular *Dragonriders of Pern* series, dragons are presented as loyal servants or, more accurately, as partners. In *Moreta: Dragonlady of Pern*, we learn that they are bonded to their human riders by a joining called Impression. "At the moment of hatching," the author tells us, "the dragon, not the rider, chooses his partner and telepathically communicates this choice to the chosen rider." This telepathic bond between dragon and human rider continues for life. McCaffrey depicts dragons as beautiful, intelligent, good creatures, and thus the primary negative impact of her novels is symbol inversion.

Ursula Le Guin deserves a category of her own, but for our purpose here (which is no more than an attempt to see the basic structure of the problem) I have included her as one of the five examples in the gray zone. Like the other authors, she has written books that are close to category 2 and some that clearly belong in category 3. Le Guin writes with such intelligence and creative power that in nearly all of her novels the reader is absorbed into worlds of compelling realism (despite the fantasy settings). Her most popular books are the Earthsea tetralogy, which is comprised of *The Wizard of Earthsea*, *The Tombs of Atuan*, *The Farthest Shore*, and *Tehanu*. In the world of Earthsea, magic is the religion and magicians are its priests. The young hero, Ged, desires the powers of wizardry and only through much trial and error learns that a true wizard is one who places his powers at the service of mankind rather than himself. In this and other matters, the author demonstrates some wise insights into human nature, but in the end the good elements in these novels are absorbed into Le Guin's gnostic view of the universe. She employs the themes of sin and redemption (without using those terms), the heroic quest, and moral struggle, yet she places them at the service of a spirituality that in reality corrupts the integrity

of the human person by making a false peace with destructive spiritual activity. Earthsea presents the universe as a dynamic system in which magic, science, and religion are merged into what is called the Great Balance or the Equilibrium. In the great balance between good and evil, all supernatural powers are merely naturalized. The resulting effect in the reader is a lowering of vigilance about the occult. By a marvellous sleight of hand, Le Guin achieves this by appearing to be a moralist. Her vision is the "broad" viewpoint, as opposed to the "narrow gate" of genuine salvation, authentic liberation, true wisdom.

Because her creative imagination is so outstanding, her intellect probing and richly textured, and her writing skills of very high quality, the reader, even a discerning adult reader, may find himself beguiled. The adolescent reader will be especially vulnerable unless he understands clearly the actual condition of the real cosmos: its spiritual warfare, its sexual conflicts, its confused thinking. Of the foregoing examples of gray-zone fantasy, Le Guin's books are the ones I would most caution the undiscerning reader to avoid. At least, they should be avoided until the young reader is firmly grounded in his faith, understands New Age misconceptions, and is intelligent enough to be able to engage the power of Le Guin's intellect. A tall order for any of us! This is not to say that the author is a dry intellectual. On the contrary—she is a superb artist, thoroughly entertaining, and this coupled with her mental powers make for a formidable adversary. An indication of how powerful she is can be found in the Christian booklists that recommend her work to young readers.

There is another point worth considering here. Le Guin's novels for adult readers are no less intriguing, though their themes are more complex. In *The Left Hand of Darkness,* for example, she explores the theme of sexual identity and makes a strong case for androgynous sexuality and bisexuality. Her approach to her "sub-created" worlds is sociological, psychological, anthropological, and "spiritual" in the Gnostic sense—a blend that is symptomatic of thinkers involved in the New Age Movement. Indeed, some of her more recent novels explore New Age ideas in a positive light. I think it very likely that as they grow older young readers hooked on Earthsea will go on to absorb more serious errors through the author they have come to admire and love.

We must ask ourselves some hard questions here: If a child's reading is habitually in the area of the supernatural, is there not a risk that he will develop an insatiable appetite for it, an appetite that grows ever stronger as it is fed. Will he be able to recognize the boundaries between spiritually sound imaginative works and the deceptive ones? Here is another key point for parents to consider: Are we committed to discussing these issues with our children? Are we willing to accompany them, year after year, as their tastes develop, advising caution here, sanctioning liberality there, each of us, young and old, learning as we go? Are we willing to pray diligently for the gift of wisdom, for inner promptings from the Holy Spirit, and for warnings from guardian angels? Are we willing to sacrifice precious time to pre-read some novels about which we may have doubts? Are we willing to invest effort to help our children choose the right kind of fantasy literature from library and bookstore? Unless we are, perhaps this entire field should be left alone for a time.

Some Notes on Spiritual Discernment

There is no infallible recipe for sorting through the mass of material that is offered to our children. Short of plunging into an exhaustive study of this field (a time-consuming and often unpleasant task), parents would do well to focus on certain principles and pray for a spirit of right discernment.

It is natural enough that parents may begin to feel more than a little concerned about the present situation. Not infrequently I have corresponded with parents who feel alarmed and shaken by it. Confusion breeds fear, and fear breeds anger. Human nature is especially prone to unjust expressions of anger when our children are threatened. I see two alternative temptations for the parent who has suddenly been alerted to the battle for his child's mind. On the one hand, a parent may be so dismayed by the sheer mass of fronts on which he must now struggle that he is tempted to dismiss the problem altogether. It is simply too much to handle, he feels. Perhaps it is a tempest in a teapot, he argues with himself. It is overreaction, it is alarmism, he concludes.

On the other hand, he may accept the fact that there is a real crisis under way and that children, moreover his children, are its potential victims. Yet, feeling unequipped to deal with it, pushed into a corner, unable to answer his children's demands for an explanation of why he rejects the questionable material, he may be tempted to an impulsive closing of all cultural doors. He may try to put his children into quarantine, permitting them access only to books, films, and other cultural material released before the 1960s.

We must understand that both approaches are going to have negative effects on our children. Clearly, we cannot surrender quietly and do nothing as the tide of evil rises. Is it not the sin of presumption to expect a divine rescue operation if we refuse to do our part? On the other hand, should we become hysterical and run about shouting, "The sky is falling! The sky is falling!"? We should ask ourselves which is the worse attitude, which will bring about the greatest harm: the psychology of "denial" (refusing to admit that anything is wrong) or the psychology of "hysteria" (becoming so alarmed that we leap for hasty solutions)? I believe that both are harmful, but I am convinced that denial is definitely worse. Denial breeds a state of blindness, a false peace with untruth, which can only deepen as the spirit of the times continues to invade our families. By contrast, no one can sustain hysteria for long, and with prayer, grace, and an effort to examine the problem in the light of reason, a proper balance can be restored.

There is a third approach. The wisdom of two thousand years of Catholicism has given us a heritage that is always at our disposal. It is called the discernment of spirits. First and foremost we must remember that we are in a spiritual war zone. Neither cowardice nor blind rage is helpful here. Understanding the tactics of our spiritual adversary is of utmost importance.

The saints have written extensively on these tactics, and equally important they urge us to avail ourselves of the help offered by the Holy Spirit and God's angels. The following are some basic principles:

1. God has chosen to create man a free being. Though the likeness of God in us was defaced by original sin, his image

within us has never been destroyed. Because of Christ's redemption, we are no longer slaves to sin but free to choose the good with the help of grace.

The devil's major tactic is to keep each of us from living in the state of sanctifying grace, to lure us into a state of mortal sin and to keep us there. When he tempts us, he fills the imagination with sensual delights, fantasies, and gratifications that are forbidden by God. At the same time the mind is drawn into rationalizations in order to justify the wrong choice. The enemy's desire is to withdraw us from the light of Christ, beginning with evil thoughts and culminating in evil acts. To combat these temptations, our guardian angels rouse within us the sting of conscience and remorse and prompt us with the light of reason.

For most of us, the imagination is a battleground where we often struggle with temptations to one or more of the deadly sins. It may take the form of lust or malice or greed or envy or other sins, but in whatever guise it comes, its primary purpose is to drag us down to destruction. God permits this struggle in order to strengthen us, to teach us to rely more completely on him and less on our own limited strengths, to instruct us, and to draw us ultimately to himself. As we mature in the life of Christ, we will not be so easily misled by what is flashed onto the screen of the imagination or by the emotions these images can sometimes rouse in us. Yet, even great saints say that this struggle will continue to some degree until death.

2. Those souls who are earnestly striving to cleanse themselves from sin and seek to live ever more perfectly in Christ are usually subjected to the opposite method. Instead of luring us with pleasurable sensations, the devil now afflicts us with anxiety, sadness, loneliness, fear, and all kinds of false reasoning that deeply disturb the soul. With this method he seeks to discourage us from advancing in faith.

To combat this tactic, the Holy Spirit and the angels prompt the soul with consolation, inspirations, bursts of courage and trust in God, and supernatural peace, thus drawing us more deeply into a life of prayer. God has determined that we should ask for what we need. We are creatures, not gods, and by learning to ask God for everything, we gradually deactivate the will to power and self-divinization that is part of fallen human nature. At the same time we learn that the Father is Love itself. He will force nothing upon us (it is the devil who strives always to force, to invade, to control us). God desires us to enter into a relationship with him that is pure love, a mutual free gift of the self. As we grow in this awareness, we learn to pray with perseverance, learn to ask for every grace, become more grateful and confident as we experience the overflowing mercy and generosity of God.

3. As the soul advances in holiness, it continues to experience periods of consolation and desolation. Consolations are interior movements of the soul by which it is inflamed with love of God, by tears of sorrow for sins, or by tears of compassion for the sufferings of Jesus. Consolations include every interior light that brings about an increase of faith, hope, and love, any joy that attracts us to God and directs us to the praise and obedient service of God.

Desolation is the opposite: a darkness of the soul, interior turmoil of spirit, a longing to return to disordered carnal pleasures, various lacks of faith, hope, and love. During periods of desolation we must not make changes or major decisions according to our thoughts and feelings at such times or abandon the good resolutions we have made during times of consolation. Hard as it may seem, we should increase our prayer, offer some penance, make increased acts of faith, hope, and love. We must persevere patiently, remembering that the consolations of God will return. God permits these periods because we are prone to lukewarmness and sometimes slide into indifference to the things of God. Also, he wishes to test the firmness of our love and to temper us as gold is tested in fire. During such periods we should ask ourselves a few straightforward questions: Do I love only when there are rewards? Do I trust God only when my life is sailing along without problems? Am I committed to being faithful unto death, no matter what the cost?

A third reason that God permits desolations is that it is necessary for us to know that we grow in sanctity only as a result of God's great generosity, not because of our own willpower, intelligence, natural virtues, or other personal qualities. To "rise up" on the wings of such false glory is a sure recipe for destruction. Pride, the greatest and the subtlest of sins, is the death-bringer.

The foregoing is only a thumbnail sketch of what the Christian spiritual writers tell us about growing in the life of the Spirit. But it is important at this point in our discussion, because when faced with a sudden awareness that the life of his family is being adversely affected by the spiritual warfare going on in the surrounding culture, a parent's faith may be put to the test. In order to meet the challenge, he will need to learn new tactics. If, for example, he discovers his child playing "Dungeons and Dragons" or fooling around with a Ouija board at a friend's home, he should recognize that his child is in extreme spiritual danger. He must act charitably but firmly to put an end to the activity. If he discovers that his child is reading questionable material or has become addicted to playing sinister video games, the danger may not be quite so immediate, but in the long run it can be just as destructive. In either situation the parent needs to know what is the best approach to take. Prudence is needed here, not passivity or panic. He must resist the temptations of denial or alarmism. He should neither brush the whole problem aside as unimportant nor fly into emotional outbursts. He should pray.

He should ask God for spiritual protection for his family (a prayer that should be made daily). He should plead for the Blood of Jesus to cover his home and each member of his family. He should ask for the protection of the holy angels to surround and fill his home and family and for special graces to be given to his children's guardian angels. He should invoke the intercession of the saints and all holy angels, including Saint Michael the Archangel, protector of the Church, the one who cast Satan out of heaven. He should pray to the Blessed Virgin Mary, Mother of God, who has been given a special role during these times as an instrument to defeat Satan's plans.

Then he should pray for the specific grace to meet this particular crisis. He should ask God for extraordinary wisdom, for the right words to say, and for the spirit in which to say them to help ensure their effectiveness. He should ask God for the force of love and peace to be in his heart as he speaks to an errant or misled child. No mountain is more difficult to move than the human will when it is determined to cling to a vice. No amount of lecturing, cajoling, or reasoning can free a child who has come to believe (in the inverted logic of sin) that his addiction is life itself. I have found that in such difficult situations, where my prayers seem to be having little or no effect (usually because sin, habits of self-indulgence, or a spirit of rebellion is involved), fasting is also necessary. Fasting is not easy. I'm not very good at it, but I have learned through personal experience that it can move mountains.

Chapter VI

The Restoration of Christian Storytelling

Because the Holy Spirit is always pouring out life upon God's people, we must never succumb to the temptation to think that the false culture has won. Despite its apparent powers, its noise, and its glamor, it is a moribund system that has not much longer to live. At every moment Jesus stands ready to restore the world and ourselves to the Father. That restoration will necessarily entail a regaining of our courage and a willingness to respond to the promptings of the Spirit, regardless of the odds that seem stacked against us.

A regeneration of Christian culture is not only possible, it is our responsibility. We bear witness to the greatest story of all, a story that, as Chesterton said, fulfills man's greatest needs. In *The Everlasting Man*, he pointed out that "the sanity of the world was restored and the soul of man offered salvation by something which did indeed satisfy the two warring tendencies of the past; which had never been satisfied in full and most certainly never satisfied together. It met the mythological search for romance by being a story and the philosophical search for truth by being a true story."[1]

The imagination was originally created to be God's territory, a faculty of man's soul that would help him to comprehend the invisible realities. Though the modern imagination has reverted

[1] *The Everlasting Man* (San Francisco: Ignatius Press, 1986), p. 380.

to the pre-Christian split in consciousness, haunted and malformed by false stories, the territory can be reclaimed. Indeed, God wants it to be fully restored to grace, and part of that restoration will demand of Christian storytellers a consecration of their own imagination to the absolute authority of the will of God, to a poverty of spirit that kneels before the source of all true creativity, asking for inspiration. The "baptized" intellect must also be about a long labor of developing its skills and understanding. Because true culture has an inherent restorative power, and furthermore because art always has an authoritative voice in the soul, we must trust that over time works of truth and beauty created from authentic spiritual sources will help to bring about a reorientation of man. It goes without saying that culture alone will not restore a society to sanity, for culture can reinforce both the good and evil impulses in man. The question we need to ask is not so much what sort of surgery should be applied to a sick body but what are the first principles of health. And in this respect, I think the classical fairy story has a great deal to teach us.

Tolkien's Middle-earth

The work of three Christian writers in the tradition of true fairy tales provides models of some of the possibilities that are open to us: J. R. R. Tolkien, C. S. Lewis, and George MacDonald. All three build their fictional worlds upon a right understanding of the moral order of the universe, and each demonstrates that a true fairy tale is more complex than the mere construction of an artificial black-and-white world. Each in his way shows us that evil can, and frequently does, disguise itself as good and that, by the same token, good is often mistaken for evil. Sorting it all out is the stuff of great drama. J. R. R. Tolkien's "Middle-earth" is not a fairyland in the cliché sense of the term. In fact it is the true realm of *Faërie*, a state of mind or being in which things become ultimately "more real", distinct, and focused into their true form. Though a "sub-creation", Middle-earth is our world. The events of the tales are situated in a fictional older time, divided into Three Ages that occurred long before any history now known to us. The First Age is described in *The Silmarillion*, a work compiled from writings Tolkien began in 1917 and constantly revised throughout his life. First published in 1977, much of it long predates the more famous works, *The Hobbit* and *The Lord of the Rings*. It is an account of "the Elder Days", the foundation of the world, composed of legends, poems, annals, and oral tales (all invented by Tolkien) through which the author portrays a vast titanic struggle between the hosts of the angels of the Creator and the fallen angels. The names and places are new to us, but the main characters are easily identifiable. The demonology and angelology are exactly Christian. The fall of man and the corruption of a beloved creation is heartbreaking; its full impact leaves the reader with a sense of horror—spiritual horror.

Tolkien's epic masterpiece, *The Lord of the Rings*, depicts the decisive events that occur at the end of the Third Age. The central character, Frodo Baggins, is a member of the gentle, small, and fun-loving people known as hobbits. He is asked by a "wizard" named Gandalf to bear a ring of diabolical power to a mountain in a kingdom ruled by the Dark Lord, Sauron, in order to destroy the ring in the volcano's fires and thus weaken the grip that Sauron has over the world. Frodo agrees to undertake this journey into darkness but soon realizes that the ring has a seductive hold over him. He is nearly crushed under its weight, a weight that increases as he comes closer to the mountain. He constantly reminds himself that he must destroy the ring so that it no longer will be a corrupting influence on the world. Yet as he progresses upon the journey, he must also face his own vulnerability to temptation.

Stratford Caldecott has written that Tolkien's ring represents pride and power: "The Ring is what draws us to the Dark Lord, by tempting us to become like him. Its circular shape expresses its nature: the will enclosed in upon itself. Its empty centre suggests the void into which we thrust ourselves by using the Ring. But if this is what the Ring represents, its renunciation is finally impossible without the help of grace."[2] Toward the climax of the story, everything is demanded of Frodo at the very moment when he is weakest. Poised on the edge of an absolute darkness that is a vision of hell, terrified, hungry, exhausted, and faltering, he faces the ultimate test. Yet the mysterious ways of divine providence are revealed at the last moment, and the ring is destroyed. Contrast this message to that of Disney's Aladdin, who goes boldly and vigorously down into darkness in order to *seize* the power for himself and is wonderfully rewarded for his efforts. The story of Frodo's quest is perhaps one of the great mythological creations of all time, and for that reason it will long outlast the more superficial fantasies of Disney studios. Its reputation continues to grow fifty years after its publication. It is about the weak and the good overcoming the powerful and the malign. It is about love, loyalty, and humility. It is about spiritual growth, chivalry, and self-sacrifice, and most of all about the real victory over the powers of darkness.

That battle begins where it always begins, with the overcoming of fear. But in a world that is growing steadily dark with foreboding, where the odds stacked against the good are mounting, where confusion, betrayal, and falsehood seem to infect the very air that is breathed, how are the weak to triumph? In *The Two Towers* (the second volume of the trilogy), one of the characters asks, "How shall a man judge what to do in such times?"

---

[2] "Lord of the Imagination" by Stratford Caldecott, in the December 1992 issue of *Second Spring*.

The hero-king Aragorn replies, "As he has ever judged. . . . Good and ill have not changed since yesteryear; nor are they one thing among Elves and Dwarves and another among Men. It is a man's part to discern them, as much in the Golden Wood as in his own house."

The discernment of the right paths that must be taken, if good is to triumph, is dramatized in the myriad geographical, emotional, spiritual, and symbolic choices faced by the questers. In each of these, Tolkien's world is faithful to the moral order of the universe, to the absolute necessity of freedom. Middle-earth is a "sacramental" world, an "incarnational" world (though these words are not used). Spirit and matter are never portrayed as dualistic adversaries but as degrees of interpenetration. Man is of one order, Elves of another, and the "wizards" such as Gandalf are of yet another order that is part material, part spiritual. Though Gandalf is a creature, he is less material than Men, Dwarves, or Elves, and especially so after his death and transformation; but neither is he a solely spiritual being like the Valar, the angelic created beings who govern the world invisibly. Tolkien has written elsewhere that Gandalf is not a "magician" like those of traditional fairy tales. He is rather a kind of moral guardian, similar to the guardian angels, but more incarnate.[3] His task is to advise, instruct, and arouse to resistance the hearts and minds of those threatened by Sauron. He does not do the work for them; they must use their natural gifts—in this we see a living image of grace building upon nature, never overwhelming nature or replacing it. Gandalf's gifts are used sparingly, and then only so far as they assist the other creatures in the exercise of their free will in their moral choices. Supernatural powers, Tolkien demonstrates

---

[3] See *The Letters of J. R. R. Tolkien*, edited by Humphrey Carpenter and Christopher Tolkien (Boston: Houghton Mifflin, 1981). In letters 155, 156, and 286, Tolkien explains his depiction of matter and spirit, the distinction between good magic and evil magic, and the nature of various beings in Middle-earth.

repeatedly, are very much a domain infested by the "deceits of the Enemy", used for domination of other creatures' free will, and as such they are metaphors of sin and spiritual bondage. By contrast, good magic in Middle-earth is never used to over-power, deceive, or defile. It always seeks to help other beings become more truly themselves, to ensure the preservation of their freedom. It is a metaphor of grace. We must also remember here that Middle-earth is a sub-creation, situated in a fictional "time" that predates Judeo-Christianity. Is the author risking a blurring of distinctions between good and evil? I do not think so. If anything, he has used fictional good magic as a way of sharpening the distinctions. He imparts crucial truths about the tactics of the enemy, and does so in a form that is intelligible to all. After plunging into this imaginary kingdom for a time, one returns to the shopping mall and the controlled hysteria of the urban freeway with an acute sense of the unreality of much of what our world calls normal. The air in that other-world is brac-ing, life is high drama, and the destiny of the human soul is the greatest adventure of all.

C. S. Lewis' Fantasy Novels

A few years ago I wrote a series of magazine articles on the role of fantasy tales in the development of children's imaginative lives, drawing mainly upon my observations and experience as a fa-ther who likes to read such stories to his children. Some of the most interesting responses I received from individual readers con-cerned the brief section in the articles dealing with the fiction of C. S. Lewis, especially his seven-volume fantasy series for chil-dren, *The Chronicles of Narnia*, and his so-called "space trilogy".

Generally, the readers' responses fell into two main categories, which could be summarized by the following statements:

a. "Although I have always admired Lewis' defense of Christian ideas, I rejected his fantasy novels as being too pagan, and possibly an unhealthy influence on my children. You have helped me to see that they are, after all, within the boundaries of Christian fiction."

b. "I do not understand why you should question a Christian apologist of such outstanding merit. This is clearly the case of a gnat biting the ankle of an elephant."

These two conflicting responses are a fair indication of the confusion that prevails among thoughtful parents trying to discern what is wholesome material for their children. Regarding the latter response, I quite agree with the proportions involved. But I did not intend to bite Lewis' ankle. I wished only to clarify my thinking on the role of symbols used in fiction. I thought, and still think, that we can only benefit by questioning even our genuine heroes about what they really intended to say to us. Lamentably, Lewis is dead, and we cannot now engage him in those dialogues, which he would no doubt have found interesting and enjoyable. But we can examine some of the themes he introduced to us, in the hope that they will throw light upon the cultural confusion that now, a generation later, afflicts the life of families to the very foundation.

Lewis was a member of an intimate circle of friends that included Tolkien, Charles Williams, and a number of writers who regularly met to discuss and to create literature. Most of them were Christians. They called themselves jestingly the "Inklings". Like many intelligent believers of their times, they were disturbed by the ominous gaps in modern education. Lewis and Tolkien believed that man could not properly understand his own era if he had little or no grasp of the cultures from which he had sprung; nor could he think rightly if he did not understand the history of ideas. Literature was a central, vital way of imparting those ideas, of meeting the minds of the past, and of developing a sense of the meaning of the human person. Lewis' discernment about "good" mythology was similar to G. K. Chesterton's—he saw in the strivings of many ancient peoples a glimmer of light, a presentiment, a yearning forward through the medium of art toward the fullness of the truth that would one day be made flesh in the Incarnation. His love for these longings in the soul of pre-Christian man prompted him to create his own mythological world, one founded, it should be noted, on the Judeo-Christian revelation.

The Chronicles of Narnia explores a world that has fallen under a curse and is in the process of being restored, through much suffering and conflict, to its original harmony. On one level these novels are tremendous adventures, and on another they are rich theological treatises that teach truth without falling into the tedious habit of preaching to children. The search for truth is simply part of the excitement. I have rarely read so clear a portrait of what religious thinkers call "spiritual warfare" and "discernment of spirits". The attempted psychological seduction of the young questers depicted in *The Silver Chair* is especially well done and could be read as a description of what is occurring right now in our own culture. In this story the crown prince of Narnia has been kidnapped and brainwashed by a powerful witch, who holds him captive in a dark underworld. The children who are the central characters of the story have gone down into the dark in order to rescue him. They too are captured by the witch, who appears to them in the form of a beautiful queen. Lewis' portrayal of her "psychology" is fascinating. She attempts to enthrall them by reprogramming their minds, while at the same time lulling their natural defenses to sleep with a drug and the mesmerizing thrumming of a mandolin:

Slowly and gravely the Witch repeated, "There is no *sun*." And they all said nothing. She repeated, in a softer and deeper voice, "There is no *sun*." After a pause and after a struggle in their minds, all four of them said together, "You are right. There is no sun." It was such a relief to give in and say it.

"There never was a *sun*," said the Witch.

"No, there never was a sun," said the Prince, and the Marsh-wiggle, and the children.[4]

They are close to utter enslavement when the brave creature, the Marsh-wiggle, deliberately burns himself in the fireplace in order to shock his mind back to reality. When he does so and challenges the witch, she reveals her true nature by taking on the form of a powerful serpent, thus alerting the children to their peril.

In *The Voyage of the Dawn Treader*, Lewis shows us that not all temptations have exterior sources. Every fall from grace requires some kind of assent from us. In this novel a band of children are on a long sea voyage and have stopped on a tropical island. One of their company, a very selfish, very modern little boy named Eustace, runs off into the interior of the island and stumbles upon a real myth. Raised in the atmosphere of the pseudo-scientific myths of his "enlightened" liberal parents, he is singularly unprepared for what happens. He meets a dragon. When the dragon dies a natural death, Eustace crawls into its lair to escape a rain storm. The narrator describes what happens next:

> Most of us know what we should expect to find in a dragon's lair, but as I said before, Eustace had read only the wrong books. They had a lot to say about exports and imports and governments and drains, but they were weak on dragons. That is why he was so puzzled at the surface

---

[4] *The Silver Chair* (New York: Macmillan, 1953), p. 152.

on which he was lying. . . . And of course Eustace found it to be what any of us could have told him in advance— treasure.[5]

Eustace, his head full of economics, crams his pockets with gold and diamonds, then falls asleep. When he wakes up he discovers to his horror that he has become a dragon. The horror fades quickly as he realizes that he has nothing to be afraid of any more. *He* has become the terror, and nothing in the world but a knight (and how many of those were there any more?) would dare to attack him. He can get even with the other children, who dislike him, who do not understand his superiority. Eustace's greed has led to pride, and pride has opened up vistas of power. Yet, Eustace, for all his faults, still has a human heart, and he is suddenly overcome with an appalling loneliness. He weeps with remorse and seeks out the company of the other children. To his surprise they treat him with sympathy and try to help him. Though they are about to embark on the continuation of their voyage, they will not abandon him. Later, the lion Aslan (the Christ-figure in the series) comes to him and leads him to a well of crystal-clear water in a beautiful garden on a mountain-top. Eustace tries to remove his dragon scales in order to go down into the well and cleanse himself of his mistake. But nothing works: he removes the dragon skin only to find more layers beneath. When Eustace finally realizes that he cannot un-dragon himself, he understands that only Aslan can free him. Eustace describes what follows:

> I was afraid of his claws, I can tell you, but I was pretty nearly desperate. So I now lay down on my back to let him do it.
>
> The very first tear he made was so deep that I thought it

5 *The Voyage of the Dawn Treader* (New York: Macmillan, 1952), p. 71.

had gone right into my heart. And when he began pulling my skin off, it hurt worse than anything I've ever felt. The only thing that made me able to bear it was just the pleasure of seeing the stuff peel off.

Aslan removes all the dragon layers and throws Eustace naked into the well. When the boy is clean, he takes him out, dresses him in new clothing, and returns him to his friends. This is salvation history, distilled in the form of Story.

There can be no doubt that Lewis was a Christian evangelist of outstanding genius. A reading of his many essays and his fiction reveals a converted soul, a heart struggling to communicate the mysteries of God, a mind awake. It is in this context that I raise a certain question with a feeling of trepidation. In many discussions with Christians—and even some non-Christians who admire Lewis for his agility of mind and his astonishing richness of imagination—I have met an unswerving loyalty to the man as a man. For many people of our generation he is a teacher and hero who merits a category all his own. The scope of his contribution to religious thought, to the defense of the Christian teachings, and to the development of Christian imagination is practically unparalleled. Not surprisingly, one of his greatest personal qualities was his humility. And that is why I expect he would have been the first to sit back with a tankard of ale before him, puffing on his pipe while happily discussing, as he did so often with his fellow Inklings, the theological merits of his literary characters. He would have enjoyed, I think, the thrust and parry of a debate over the symbolic meaning of his sub-creation.

Against the background of the collapse of the symbolic life of Western culture, the use of certain imagery in his work takes on a new significance. And it is in this light that I think a note of caution is needed. Lewis was heir to a rich intellectual past. Like Tolkien, he taught at Oxford, and later he was professor of

Medieval and Renaissance English at Cambridge. He was nurtured in two great cultural centers of the world, environments that valued literature of practically any sort as a priceless heritage of the human community. He was a man in love with language, lore, fable, and history. That his primary love was Christ only increased his desire to reconcile the old pre-Christian literary world with the new. Thus, he did not regard an imaginative mingling of the two worlds as presenting any serious difficulty.

In the Narnia books, for example, the author attempts to "baptize" the ancient classical pagan mythologies and depicts fauns and satyrs, naiads and dryads, as full citizens in the Kingdom of God. His attempt to explain classical mythology from a Christian perspective is heroic, but unless properly understood it can lead the reader, especially the young child, to some misconceptions. Although Narnia is a sub-creation, we must ask what is being communicated in it regarding classical paganism—a question that is best answered by a reading of Lewis' *Till We Have Faces*, which I will consider at greater length farther on in this chapter.

In the Narnia series Lewis intends to say that all creatures, even those that are imperfect and fallen in one world, might be unfallen in another and, by inference, might be restored to grace in our own through Christ. He is making a very important point about the creativity of God. In another universe, or on another planet, God easily could have chosen to make fauns and satyrs and centaurs. The forms of creaturehood might be different from ours, but the moral order of any and all universes God chose to create would remain the same. Thus, when the cabbie and his wife, who are transported from London to Narnia (in *The Magician's Nephew*), are anointed king and queen of Narnia after its restoration to grace, they are surrounded by a vast number of rather extraordinary subjects. The cabbie and his wife have been chosen by Aslan because of their purity of heart and nobility of character. Their subjects (bizarre as some of them may be) have chosen to reject evil and embrace good. The forms of the flesh may greatly differ, Lewis is illustrating, but the nature of good and evil does not. For this reason, I believe that the Narnia series remains within the parameters of authentic Christian sub-creation.

In Lewis' space trilogy, which includes the novels *Out of the Silent Planet, Voyage to Venus* (titled *Perelandra* in some countries), and *That Hideous Strength,* he again depicts the cosmic battle between good and evil. This is Narnia for grown-ups—although I should add that many a young reader will find much of interest in it. For sheer majesty of vision and beauty of language, this cycle of novels has few equals in its genre. Lewis' grasp of the meaning of culture is masterful. His insight into spiritual warfare is far-reaching and brilliant—one might even say prophetic. He portrays the planets of our solar system as ruled by the archangels of God, called *eldila.* Only the Earth is in darkness, besieged by a fallen *eldil,* a "black archon", who seeks to spread his dominion throughout the universe, planet by planet. Beginning with Satan's foiled attempt to overcome the planet Mars, proceeding through his attempt to bring about another fall of man on Venus, and culminating in his effort to subdue the entire planet Earth, the author symbolically traces salvation history from Genesis through to the Apocalypse.

"Who is to confound the designs of the rebel angels?" Lewis asks. It is the humble of the earth, men such as Ransom, the central character of the trilogy, working together with the angels of God. In one of the opening scenes of *Perelandra,* Ransom informs the narrator of the story (Lewis himself) that he is being called by an archangel to journey to Venus in order to fight the devil, who is planning an assault on that planet. The narrator protests, struggling helplessly for arguments to change Ransom's mind. Ransom replies:

"I know!" said he with one of his singularly disarming smiles. "You are feeling the absurdity of it. Dr. Elwin Ransom setting out single-handed to combat powers and principalities. You may even be wondering if I've got megalomania."

"I didn't mean that quite," said I.

"Oh but I think you did. At any rate that is what I have been feeling myself since the thing was sprung on me. But when you come to think of it, is it any odder than what all of us have to do every day? When the Bible used that very expression about fighting with principalities and powers and depraved hypersomatic beings at great heights . . . it meant that quite ordinary people were to do the fighting."[6]

[6] *Perelandra*, in *The Cosmic Trilogy* (London: Pan Books, 1989), p. 162.

Ransom explains that it is not a case of spiritual pride to think that humans should fight the devil on levels of combat that are ordinary *and* extraordinary. It is a case of understanding the nature of the war. The war, he explains, is changing rapidly.

> Now your idea that ordinary people will never have to meet the Dark Eldila in any form except a psychological or moral form—as temptations or the like—is simply an idea that held good for a certain phase of the cosmic war: the phase of the great siege, the phase which gave our planet its name of Thulcandra, the silent planet. But supposing that phase is passing? In the next phase it may be anyone's job to meet them . . . well, in some quite different mode.

In a long dialogue between Ransom and the scientist Weston (who is the devil's agent for the seduction of the planet Venus), Lewis outlines what so often happens to a mind without God. During his attempted plundering of Mars, Weston had been a materialist with no spiritual sensibilities whatsoever. Now, on Venus, he has "repented" of this limited viewpoint and has become colossally, ambitiously spiritual, yet he lacks understanding of the true structure of reality; he remains ignorant of the war between good and evil. Weston styles himself as one who has risen above the pathetic "myths" of Judeo-Christianity. He is now a visionary of cosmic proportions. He is no longer "narrow". He has become so "broad" that he incorporates both Satan and God into his theory of the impersonal Life-Force, which he believes is the true dynamism determining all existence, including human history. He is so "spiritual", in fact, that he becomes fertile soil for diabolical possession.

Lewis is here enfleshing in dramatic form Chesterton's insight: When man abandons genuine faith, he does not thereafter believe in nothing; he then becomes capable of believing anything.

Lewis is probing the core of a deception that is central to the crisis of our times. Modern man, he demonstrates, does not become free and superior by abandoning authentic faith as if discarding a myth; rather, he makes himself vulnerable to the most destructive myths of all.

While reading this novel aloud to three of our children a few years ago, I had quite a startling education in how perceptive the young can be. The two older girls, ages eleven and thirteen, delighted in the rich theological landscape, enjoying the story immensely, understanding most of it. They grudgingly allowed their seven-year-old brother, Ben, to sit in as long as he promised to be quiet, to refrain from interrupting with questions while I was reading. Not wanting to be banished from the room, he obediently kept silent, content to draw pictures with the crayons and paper I had given him. Exercising heroic restraint, he said not a word night after night. I was certain that he understood little of the narrative and nothing of the spiritual and intellectual concepts in the more abstract sections of the dialogue.

As I read the section where Weston tries to convince Ransom of his new "vision", I noticed Ben's growing tension. Finally, unable to contain himself, he cried:

"Careful, girls!" (Ben raised a finger of warning.) "Weston is a New-Ager!"

We all stared at him and burst out laughing.

Ben underlined for me an urgent problem faced by parents in these times, and in doing so he contributed to the writing of this book by making me ask myself: Have I sufficiently grasped the fact that children absorb a lot more than we think they do? Have I taken sufficient care in assessing the material I give them? Most of us would probably answer yes to that question, because conscientious parents are fairly aware of the sad state of the culture, and have responded with a certain vigilance. But, I must admit that my own vigilance has been a hit-and-miss affair. It has not been difficult to recognize the obvious assaults upon the young mind, and with a little prayer and previewing I have learned to weed out the less obvious invasions of the child's imagination. But beyond that I tend to get lost in confusion. It was this confusion that first prompted me to make a rough division of the field of children's culture into the four main categories discussed on page 86.

I would place the first two volumes of Lewis' "space trilogy" in category 1, material that is wholly good. Yet after three rereadings of the final novel, *That Hideous Strength*, I am still unsure where to place it on the scale. If pressed for a decision, I would probably put it somewhere just a hair below wholly good and closer to 2, fundamentally good but disordered in some details. This is not to say that Lewis' intentions in the third volume were not wholly good. They were indeed the highest. Nor is this to say that the book isn't brilliant, evangelical, wise, and prophetic. It is all of that. However, because of its extraordinary high quality, there is a particular need to reflect on a certain ambiguity in the story. This ambiguity may throw light on some of the problems we will face if we hope to restore culture.[7]

The trilogy is a true Christian classic, and I would not wish to spoil it for the reader by giving away much of the plot. However, in the final "apocalypse" Lewis introduces an element that I believe crosses over the boundaries of prudence and that needs some discussion. In their last desperate attempt to resist the Antichrist, the fictional characters are aided by the medieval magician Merlin, who is awakened from his grave (it is never explained how) for the battle with the devil. Although in some older versions of

[7] For a penetrating study of the fiction of C. S. Lewis, I urge the reader to obtain a copy of *C. S. Lewis: Man of Letters*, by Thomas Howard (San Francisco: Ignatius Press, 1987). I also recommend *C. S. Lewis for the Third Millennium*, by Peter Kreeft (San Francisco: Ignatius Press, 1994), and *The Man Who Created Narnia*, by Michael Coren (Toronto: Lester Publishing, 1994).

the Arthurian legend Merlin is portrayed as a Christian, he is in modern accounts almost always portrayed as a Druid or a Gnostic of some sort. Lewis portrays him as a vague mixture of Druid and Christian. Is his motive no more than a literate Englishman's affection for the romance of his past, perhaps even a nostalgia for the stories that thrilled his imagination as a child? If so, we might ask if this has proved to be wise, considering the neopagan inroads made into modern literature during the decades since the book was first published. Several fiction writers belonging to the generation that came after Lewis have devoted themselves with talent and passion to resurrecting the Arthurian legend, of which Merlin was a central figure. Although some have written about that period from the Christian view of things, most have characterized Merlin as an embodiment of the "broad" personality, one who bridges the gap between the "narrow" restrictions of Christianity and the lush arcane knowledge of the pagan world. Merlin is the magus, the knower, crafty and wise, a reconciler of darkness and light. Can a young reader of the neopagan versions of the legend fail to be imbued with a sense that the Gnostic cosmos seems so much more fascinating and rewarding than the Christian?

That Hideous Strength is no advertisement for neopaganism, yet there are elements in it that lend themselves to a neopagan interpretation of the story. Although Lewis' Merlin is a sketchy character, he is definitely presented as a magician, as a man who employs occult powers, even though he says many a thing that would indicate he acknowledges the Christian God. What is he, then? Perhaps a "Christian Gnostic"? He fights the devil, and who could fault him for that? But he does so with the powers of the Old Age. What is Lewis trying to say here? That more things can be baptized than we suspect? That the pagan magicians would be true believers if given a second chance? That they lived in a more innocent age? Perhaps he does intend to say this, because when Merlin offers to employ his powers in the service of the good, Ransom refuses, explaining to him: "Your weapon would break in your hands. For the Hideous Strength confronts us, and it is as in the days when Nimrod built the tower to reach heaven."

"Hidden it may be," Merlin replies, "but not *changed*. Leave me to work, Lord. I will wake it."

"No," says Ransom, "I forbid it. Whatever of spirit may linger in the earth has withdrawn fifteen hundred years further away from us since your time. You shall not lift your little finger to call it up. It is in this age utterly unlawful."[8]

But was it ever lawful in the eyes of God, ever innocent? "It was never *very* lawful", Ransom adds, then goes on to explain that one of the reasons Merlin was awakened was so that his own soul should be saved. Ransom has said the moral thing, of course, but later in the story, when Merlin does use his powers, we are left puzzled about why God would choose to preserve this old Druid, awakening him for the purpose of being a decisive instrument in the battle against the Gnostics of Belbury, the scientific institute that is the seat of the devil's beachhead on Earth. Was Christianity insufficient for the battle? This question is never answered.

The Christian alliance with Merlin is explained by the need to reach him first, thus averting the horrible prospect of the Belbury scientists turning him to their dark purposes. Lewis is prophetic in this insight, because an alliance between science and Gnostic mysticism would not become a significant social force until almost two decades after his death. Modern science arose from rationalism, and because it was unable to come to terms with the supernatural, to understand the subsidiary place of knowledge in the hierarchy of truth, it remained vulnerable to the seductions of irrational "knowledge". Despair of objective

---

[8] *That Hideous Strength* (London: Pan Books, 1969), p. 176.

truth would increase, and fascination with secret "knowledge" would increase along with it, until eventually science would ally itself with the will to power, which in the end leads to the dark powers of magic. But unlike the cultic pagan, the scientist would think himself the absolute master of such powers. Lewis is saying that old pagan man, for all his faults, was closer to true religion than the cold, rationalist Gnostic, who bends the knee before nothing outside his own will. The ignorant old pagan might offer a human sacrifice to placate the higher powers, but the educated new pagan could destroy an entire world in his attempt to enthrone himself. The point Lewis makes here is of great importance. The problem lies in how it is expressed.

In *That Hideous Strength,* the devil is depicted as having commandeered the powers of the state and science, money and knowledge. The author lines up against it the world of myth, nature, sexuality, intuition, and faith. These battlelines may well prove to be somewhat simplistic and even confused in comparison to that real apocalypse in which mankind will eventually be put to the test. Even so, he does us the good service of asking some pressing questions, such as: Is the spiritual, cultural, and intellectual condition of modern man ripe for the reign of the Antichrist? And, are Christians in fit condition to resist him? While Lewis never gives away his personal viewpoint on the matter—whether he thinks this century is the time of the end or merely a dress rehearsal—he does urge us to look around with awareness and to ask the vital questions.

Toward the end of the book in a chapter titled "The Descent of the Gods", five "gods" come to visit Ransom and Merlin as they prepare to fight the decisive battle with the forces of darkness. Mercury, Venus, Mars, Saturn, and Jupiter—the spirits of their respective unfallen planets—are servants of the one true God. Ransom and Merlin are "caught up in the *Gloria* which those five excellent Natures perpetually sing. . . ." In Lewis' fictional universe all the powers of nature (except Earth's) exist in right order, exercising their purpose in perfect harmony with the will of their Creator. The earthly pagan myths about the gods, Lewis implies, are blurred intuitions about real angelic and demonic beings. As the angelic "gods" radiate their power, Ransom and Merlin are transfigured, immersed in the glory of the heavens, and strengthened for the battle. The author intends to say, with Saint Paul, that "all of creation is groaning in one great act of giving birth." Man can neither abandon nor reject nature; matter is neither to be escaped nor despised. Rather it is to be restored to the Father through Christ.

Just how that restoration is to take place is not always clear in the trilogy. At the climax of the final novel, Merlin arrives at Belbury. There, he is present at a banquet where scientists, journalists, politicians, and various other influential people have gathered to learn more about the new world order. The banquet collapses into a second Tower of Babel as the participants begin to babble incoherently and dissolve into a shouting, hysterical mob. A gun is drawn, shots are fired, pandemonium breaks out, people scream and stampede toward the exits. Is this God's doing or Merlin's magic? We never find out.

Worse follows: the animals in the institute's zoo, victims of the scientists' experiments, are sent by Merlin to the dining room, "maddened by his voice and touch". Snakes, wolves, tigers, and an elephant run amok, killing most of the guests in the room. The few leaders who escape, now fully controlled by their demonic masters, choose various forms of self-destruction.

"In fighting those who serve devils," Ransom says, "one always has this on one's side: their Masters hate them as much as they hate us. The moment we disable the human pawns enough to make them useless to Hell, their own Masters finish the work for us. They break their tools."

After the demise of Belbury and all its works, the good gather for a final discussion, trying to come to some understanding of what has happened. One of the characters, a reformed skeptic, says:

"All this has the disadvantage of being contrary to the observed laws of Nature."

"It is not contrary to the laws of nature", replies another, ". . . the laws of the universe are never broken. Your mistake is to think that the little regularities we have observed on our planet for a few hundred years are the real unbreakable laws; whereas they are only the remote results which the true laws bring about more often than not as a kind of accident."

"Shakespeare never breaks the real laws of poetry", a third character points out. "But by following them he breaks every now and then the little regularities which critics mistake for the real laws."

Lewis seems to be saying two things here: The first is quite true, that we can too easily mistake the disorders of a fallen civilization as fixed principles, and we can assume wrongly that our world is all there is. Unless we have a truly cosmic vision of God's universal principles, we can be deceived, we can mistake the part (and a very damaged part it is) for the whole. We can think that a culture of corruption and death is the norm.

The second implication in the foregoing dialogue is more problematic. Is Lewis saying that God's principles are not violated when occult powers are harnessed for the purpose of serving good ends? Is he saying that this is merely a breaking of "little regularities"? What, then, does he make of the severe and repeated scriptural warnings against involvement in the occult?

There is ample evidence that Lewis understands the dangers. For example, in *The Magician's Nephew*, the first novel of the Narnia series, the corruption of Narnia is brought about by an elderly gentleman of London, the magician of the novel's title, who enjoys dabbling in the occult. He uses rings of power to open the door between worlds, and inadvertently his nephew steps through, setting off a chain of events that bring war to an innocent planet. Clearly, the author recognizes that there is a "war in the heavens" and that both sides seek to influence mankind. However, in *That Hideous Strength*, it appears that he has made a distinction between the invisible warfare of this present darkness and the occult powers of the pre-Christian cultic pagans. He says that those powers were unenlightened and are now forbidden, but does he really say enough? The uneducated reader, especially the young reader, could easily misinterpret Lewis' meaning and jump to the conclusion that occult powers need only a few corrective measures in order to be brought into the divine order of creation. It is precisely this ambiguity that leaves room for the invasion of the imagination—a development Lewis probably did not foresee.

The trilogy is a stunningly prophetic work on the whole, and thus one wonders about this lapse in clarity. Perhaps at the time he wrote it Lewis considered the rampant growth of secularism, and the resulting dehumanization of the West, as our primary danger, the seedbed of worse disorders to come. Impelled by an urgent sense that mankind was being seduced by the tragically stunted materialistic world view, he may have intended to recall his readers to a sense of mystery and wonder. By using magic as a metaphor, he probably wished to remind us of the spiritual dimension of existence, pointing, as he so often did, to the largeness and complexity of the universe.

Tolkien and Lewis disagreed with each other about the right use of fantasy and myth, a more or less friendly controversy that went on for some time. Prompted by a discussion in 1931, Tolkien wrote his poem "Mythopoeia" in answer to Lewis' remark that myths are "lies and therefore worthless, even though breathed through silver".[9] At the time, Lewis had rejected atheism but had

---

[9] See Humphrey Carpenter's *The Inklings* (London: Allen & Unwin, 1978), pp. 42–45.

not yet become a Christian. He saw culture primarily in terms of words and ideas, a view that derived in part from the prevailing ethos of his native Northern Ireland—a Protestantism based on the primacy of the *word*. During childhood and youth Lewis had immersed himself in readings of the Norse myths, but his experience of these had more to do with evocative feelings and the thrill of narrative adventure than with the search for absolute truths. By saying that myths were lies, he was not suggesting that myths were necessarily deceptions, rather that they were irrelevant to the world of suffering he saw all around him. He was struggling with the question of the historical truth of the Gospels and was asking indirectly if the Christian story was just mythmaking, a story that might express certain ideals but one that was not literally true.

Tolkien replied that the story of the "dying god", well known to many ancient cultures, was indeed a myth, but in Christ the *real* dying God had appeared in the flesh. The prefiguring myths had become fact, and the fact still retained the character of myth. *This* Story had been written and incarnated by God himself. The insight hit Lewis like a revelation, and it was instrumental in his conversion to Christianity shortly thereafter. Eventually he became a member of the Church of England.[10] Tolkien, a devout Catholic, felt regret that Lewis never went all the way to Rome and perhaps saw in his friend's reticence a certain clinging to autonomy, a fear of placing himself under any binding authority.

[10] Lewis was baptized in the Church of Ireland. Though he later denied that his early outlook was Puritan, as a child he despised those congregations that were too "Romish" in sacraments and liturgy. Long after his adult conversion, he was not above making insensitive anti-Catholic comments, and he leaned more to the evangelical side of Anglicanism (see *The Inklings*, pp. 50–51). I refer to this only to suggest a possible source of the difference between Tolkien's and Lewis' incarnational viewpoints. Both men were consummate masters of language (the word), and both were incarnational Christians (sacrament as word), but Tolkien was more so.

As Lewis' Christian apologetics gained prominence, and converts to Christ, Tolkien could not help but admire what God was doing through the man but perhaps felt some suspicion that his friend's character retained something of the romantic individualist (a Christian version)—the solitary quester, the Norse hero battling the ice, the monsters, and the devils of the modern age. In later years he would say that vestiges of "dualism" were still cropping up in Lewis' thought. And he was never entirely happy with how myth was used in the Narnia books and the space trilogy.

Even so, the original insight about myth continued to play an important role in Lewis' developing ideas. His understanding of its power is stated most clearly in *Till We Have Faces*, first published in 1956, eleven years after the publication of *That Hideous Strength*. In this modern retelling of the Greek myth of Cupid and Psyche, he articulates the difference between cultic paganism, classical paganism, and the Christian view of man's spiritual journey. The story is narrated by an old woman named Orual, the queen of Glome (an imaginary ancient kingdom in the Middle East), who as the story begins is reflecting back on her life. Orual was born with an unlovely face; so ugly is she, in fact, that for most of her life she hides her face behind a veil. Her younger half sister, Psyche, is so beautiful and good that the common folk of Glome begin to reverence the child as a goddess. Orual loves Psyche very much but resents her as well. As the two princesses grow to womanhood, the love and the possessiveness in Orual's heart increase. She is sensitive to injustice, but she is also willful and somewhat self-righteous. Though she is maternal, brave, and capable of heroic self-sacrifice, she is unloved and often treated with disdain, while Psyche grows ever more beloved by their father and by the people of the land. It is clear enough to Orual that life is not fair. Only Psyche loves her, and Orual clings to her love ferociously.

Within the tale there is a vitally important dialogue between the classical pagan world view and the cultic. The classical pagan is represented by the girls' Greek tutor, the Fox, who is a slave and a philosopher. Speaking in tones of unswerving reasonableness, he maintains the position of the rationalist that myths are merely symbols and poetry. The cultic world view is represented by the high priest of the religion of Glome, who serves a faceless, primitive idol named Ungit. When the kingdom is endangered, Ungit needs human blood as a sacrifice. At this point the diabolical nature of cultic paganism manifests itself in earnest. The people, manipulated by Ungit's high priest, turn upon their beloved Psyche and give her to the idol as the Great Offering, the sacrifice, for she is the best they can offer. She is chained to a tree on a mountain height and abandoned there to be devoured by Ungit's son, the monstrous Shadowbrute, who is the personification of the worst terrors lurking in the imaginations of this superstitious people. She will become his Spouse, and he will destroy her as the act of consummation. "The loving and devouring are all the same thing", says the priest of Ungit. In the religion of Glome, "holiness and horror" are inextricably bound together. The Fox's view that reason and stoic piety are the more correct religious outlook, proves ineffectual—he cannot stop the horrible sacrifice that is about to take place. Neither he nor the priest is entirely right, Lewis will demonstrate, and neither is entirely wrong; indeed, the faceless, carnivorous Ungit is but a savage version of the refined Aphrodite of the Greeks.

Some time later Orual returns to the mountain to collect her sister's bones. Overcome with grief, she arrives at the place of sacrifice only to find that the remains are not there, though the chains are still wrapped around the tree. Shortly thereafter she comes upon Psyche, alive and radiantly happy. Psyche informs Orual that she was rescued by a mysterious "god", who took her to his beautiful palace, where he cares for her and feeds her—she can see and touch the palace and taste its food, but her rescuer remains invisible. She saw him only once, in a flash, when he pulled her from her chains, and though his form was indefinable, she knew that it was glorious, that *it* was a *he*. In the presence of that glory she felt only shame for her poor human nature, her mortality. Yet she soon came to know that he is purest love. Since then she has never seen him face to face, but she lives because of his love. His palace is hers, for she is his wife. Psyche calls him the Bridegroom.

Orual is shocked and says, "If this is all true, I've been wrong all my life. Everything has to be begun over again."

Psyche goes on to explain that the Bridegroom comes to their bed chamber only at night. He has told her that she must not see his face or know his name—at least not yet; she must never bring a light into the chamber.

Psyche pleads with Orual to join her, but Orual cannot see anything that Psyche describes. She recoils in unbelief. She cannot cross over into Psyche's new world, nor can she bear to lose her. She convinces herself that Psyche must be mad, merely suffering delusions as a result of her ordeal. When Psyche refuses to leave the mountain, Orual returns to the palace in the city of Glome. At first she wonders who rescued Psyche, then concludes that it must have been the "monster", the Brute. Later, the Fox scoffs at her primitive superstitions and suggests that the so-called "Bridegroom" is actually a human, one of the "vagabonds, broken men, outlaws and thieves" who live in the wilds. Orual adds that it might be "some murderer, traitor, runaway slave, or other filth". She tells the Fox that if that is the case it would be better for Psyche to die and that she, Orual, will kill her. This would be the most merciful thing to do, she believes. The Fox protests:

"There's one part love in your heart, and five parts anger, and seven parts pride."

Orual returns to the mountain with a plan. Hoping to shock

Psyche out of the delusion, she proposes a test of this invisible "god", believing that when Psyche sees him for what he is, she will return to sanity. If the plan fails, she will kill her in order to "save" her from further suffering. Orual wounds herself with a knife and threatens to kill herself and Psyche if Psyche does not go along with the test. Psyche is not afraid of death, but her love for Orual is so great that she is tormented into considering the plan. Orual gives her a lamp and oil and tells her that when the Bridegroom comes into their chamber, she must light the lamp. Like Adam and Eve, Psyche must choose whether or not to obey her Bridegroom in the darkness of absolute faith. In the end she chooses to obey Orual, thinking that by doing so she can save Orual and prove to her the beauty and nobility of her Bridegroom.

That night, Orual watches from a distance and sees the lamp being lit. It is swiftly extinguished. Suddenly the mountain is illumined by a sustained lightning flash that shines "bright and still, a homelike thing in that wild place. And for a time longer than I had expected, it shone and was still, and the whole world was still around it. Then the stillness broke." A great voice utters "strong, soaring incomprehensible speech", followed by a woman's sobs. Thunder and earthquake follow, and the sound of a crashing palace. "Something like a man" appears above Orual in a final flash of light, his face shockingly beautiful. Looking at her gravely, but without anger, he says, "Now Psyche goes out in exile. Now she must hunger and thirst and tread hard roads. Those against whom I cannot fight must do their will upon her. You, woman, shall know yourself and your work. You also shall be Psyche."

When the voice and the light cease, there is only darkness and the sound of Psyche's heartbroken weeping. Psyche goes out into exile, and Orual returns to the palace of Glome, never again to meet her beloved sister on this earth.

The remainder of the book chronicles Orual's many trials and sorrows as she faces a stream of events that challenge her to accept self-knowledge. The learning is long and hard, for Orual resists the truth. She will not accept blame for what she has done. She insists that the gods, not she, are guilty. They have denied her beauty; they have denied her the normal blessings of humble human happiness; they have denied her the love of a husband and family; they have even taken her only love, Psyche. They have left her the queenship, but in this she finds no joy. Life is absolutely unfair and burdensome. Still, Orual's good qualities come to the fore. In the long years of her reign she transforms Glome into a more sane kingdom, ruling with courage, prudence, and justice, and reducing the barbarity of the cult of Ungit. Nothing, however, gives her happiness. As her life progresses to old age, she amasses an enormous indictment against the gods.

During one of her journeys as queen, Orual stops in a foreign land and enters the temple of a new cult. Inside, she learns that the cult has sprung up around the legend of Psyche and her Bridegroom, though Orual realizes that the names of the characters have been changed and the events have been distorted by mythologizing. According to the myth, Orual is the wicked sister who ruins the life of the beautiful princess. Orual, who has given little thought to the gods for some time, is now bitterly reminded of their power over men's imaginations. This is yet one more of their cruel blows—they not only steal Psyche from Orual, they blame Orual for it!

"Now, instantly, I knew I was facing them—I with no strength and they with all; I visible to them, they invisible to me; I easily wounded (already so wounded that all my life had been but a hiding and staunching of the wound), they invulnerable; I one, they many."[11]

---

[11] *Till We Have Faces* (London: Geoffrey Bles, 1956), p. 254.

The god's last words, *You also shall be Psyche*, haunt her, but she cannot decipher what they mean. Near the climax of the tale, she has a dream in which her father, the dead king, appears to her and leads her to a mirror. He forces her to look into the mirror, and there she sees that her own face is the face of Ungit.

"Who is Ungit?" asks the king.

"I am Ungit", Orual wails. She awakes, takes up a sword, and tries to kill herself but does not have the physical strength to do it. Again she tries to kill herself, this time by drowning. But a voice booms from beyond the river, "Do not do it."

Orual recognizes it as a god's voice. "You cannot escape Ungit by going to the deadlands," says the god, "for she is there also. Die before you die. There is no chance after."

What does he mean, *die before you die*?

"Lord, I am Ungit", she cries. But there is no answer. She accepts to live for a time with this hateful knowledge of her own darkness, struggling to be as unlike Ungit as she can, hoping through Greek philosophy to "change my ugly soul into a fair one". She wants the gods to help her, but they do not. Unfairness mounts upon unfairness. She despairs that she will never cease to be like Ungit yet consoles herself with the thought that at least she had loved Psyche truly. The disaster on the mountain, so many years ago, had been the gods' fault, not hers. Indeed, everything has been the gods' fault.

In the final moments of the story, Orual has a vision in which she is bodily present. She is led into a heavenly court, where she brings her case against the gods before a judge. She is stripped naked before the eyes of the judge and a great assembly of witnesses. The agonies of her heart erupt as she hurls her grievance against the gods, the core experience of her life: her love for, and her loss of, Psyche.

"She was mine", Orual cries. "*Mine*; do you not know what that word means? Mine! You're thieves, seducers. That's my wrong.

I'll not complain (not now) that you're blood-drinkers and man-eaters. I'm past that. . . ."

Orual knows that the superstitious idols of primitive religion are reflections of the Ungit within man himself; she knows that the gods are beautiful. But that makes it a thousand times worse, she declares. The gods have everything, and Orual has nothing! Why, then, did they steal her only treasure?

Digging deep into the relationship between God and creature, Orual has voiced the fundamental protest of fallen man: that we do not know enough, do not have enough power, enough beauty, enough love, enough glory—and in all of this there is the underlying scream of protest, *that we are not God!*

Over and over Orual reads and rereads her grievance, until finally the judge says, "Enough." There is silence in the court, long enough for Orual to read her grievance aloud one more time. When she is finished there is another silence, then the judge speaks at last:

"Are you answered?" he asks.

"Yes", she replies, for at that very moment Orual realizes what she has been doing. The judge has allowed her to hear the sound of her real voice and, in the hearing, to know herself for the first time. The complaint was the answer. To have heard herself making it was to be answered. The gods she has hated are so beautiful and good and true that her accusations against them are exposed for the falsehoods they are. Their faces are radiant with glory, and this glory is their answer to all the agonized protests of man about the meaning of human suffering. For the radiant beauty of the gods is what *we* are to become, what they *desire* us to become. They are the true face of man, but man cannot find his own true face until he first recognizes the Ungit within himself.

From that point on, Orual becomes teachable, and she is led through more visions, which reveal the meaning of her life and the ultimate purpose of divine intervention in human affairs. The final vision culminates in a reunion of Psyche and Orual, who stand face to face in Psyche's heavenly House. There, Psyche is "a thousand times more her self than she had been before the Offering". Orual too has become beautiful and filled with joy; together they await the coming of the Bridegroom, who is to judge Orual. When he arrives, "dreadful and most beautiful", his judgment is mercy:

"You also are Psyche", he cries in his great voice.

The vision complete, Orual comes to herself in her own palace gardens and dies shortly after.

Of the many books Lewis wrote, this was his favorite and the one he considered to be his best. It expressed the central concerns of his life: the restoration of the image and likeness of God in man; the need for man to die in order to be reborn to his truest self; the necessity of a sometimes long process of dying, dying especially to false images of the self—the urgency of our need to accept the whole truth about ourselves. No true love is possible, Lewis demonstrates, until we abandon our claims, our rights, our grievances. Until then we will be trapped in the obscurity of our heart's mixed motives, our will to possess, to control, to be our own gods. Until then, we will continue to render down the miraculousness of existence into a world of one-dimensional objects; even the objects of our love will remain things to be consumed, regardless of how great our romantic notions and heroism may appear to us. We are all like Orual, protected by layers of pride, our innermost natures hidden even from our own eyes. In our sufferings we are stripped and recreated; only through them do we come to our senses and embrace humility. And only through humility do we begin to understand the real nature of love. We learn that God is unspeakably beautiful, and he is present. If he seems invisible, it is because we are blind; if he seems silent, it is because we are deaf. He does not answer our every question because we cannot yet understand the answer. As Orual says in the final chapter:

> Often when he was teaching me to write in Greek the Fox would say, "Child, to say the very thing you mean, the whole of it . . . that's the whole art and joy of words." A glib saying. When the time comes to you at which you will be forced at last to utter the speech which has lain at the centre of your soul for years, which you have, all that time, idiot-like, been saying over and over again, you'll not talk about joy of words. I saw well why the gods do not speak to us openly, nor let us answer. Till that word can be dug out of us, why should they hear the babble that we think we mean? How can they meet us face to face till we have faces?[12]

George MacDonald and the Baptized Dream

Lewis understood that the modern era was awash with words and that a great deal of it was clever babble. The theme of the deadliness of pride runs through much of his writing and is indicative of how careful he was to avoid being deceived by its many false faces. He was critical of himself, ever willing to see his own faults and failings, and was able to adjust his ideas where they did not match reality. Nor did he hesitate to apply critical discernment to other writers. His great gift of charity, indeed, his strong sense that *caritas* was the real antidote to *hubris*, precluded any violent swings of the axe. Instead, he employed the gentle but firm pressure of the scalpel, easing the pain with humor. Even devout Christian writers were not exempt from his surgery.

[12] Ibid., p. 305.

Lewis greatly admired the nineteenth-century Scottish Calvinist writer George MacDonald, who wrote a number of traditional fairy tales, including novels about a boy named Curdie, whose battles with evil creatures living in the underworld provided some of the inspiration for Lewis' Narnia. MacDonald's most important contribution to children's literature, however, is to be found in two novels that are solidly within the tradition of *Faërie* but that are unprecedented in their theological depth and imaginative power: *Phantastes* (published in 1858) and *Lilith* (published in 1895). In his preface to an anthology of MacDonald's writing, Lewis wrote of these two novels that they were a unique form of fantasy that "hovers between the allegorical and the mythopoeic" (mythmaking). As a young man Lewis had first encountered MacDonald's writing when he stumbled upon *Phantastes* in a book stall. At the time he had not yet become a Christian and was deeply immersed in Norse romanticism, but he recognized in *Phantastes* an imaginative world that he had never before encountered. As he read it, he realized that, "I had crossed a great frontier. I had already been waist deep in Romanticism, and likely enough, at any moment, to flounder into its darker and more evil forms, slithering down the steep descent that leads from the love of strangeness to that of eccentricity and thence to that of perversity."

The book showed the young Lewis that there were more possibilities for the life of the imagination than he had suspected. There was an invigorating joy, innocence, and even a kind of new romanticism in MacDonald's myth that had the unmistakable ring of truth. The moral universe, MacDonald showed him, was far from dull; indeed, it might be the greatest adventure of all. Lewis' conversion to Christianity did not take place until many years after this encounter, but the preparation had begun. He was later to write of *Phantastes*: "What it actually did to me was to convert . . . even to baptize my imagination. It did nothing to my intellect nor (at that time) to my conscience. Their turn came far later and with the help of many other books and men. But when the process was complete . . . I found that I was still with MacDonald and that he had accompanied me all the way." The quality that had enchanted Lewis in MacDonald's imaginative works was, in fact, the quality of the real universe, "the divine, magical, terrifying and ecstatic reality in which we all live. . . . I should have been shocked in my teens if anyone had told me that what I learned to love in *Phantastes* was goodness."

Subtitled *A Faerie Romance,* it is the tale of a man named Anodos who enters the realm of "Fairy Land" and there, through a series of fantastic events, comes to greater self-knowledge and spiritual growth. It is a tale about romance, illusion, self-delusion, and death. Above all, Anodos seeks love, and he encounters many of its faces: romantic passion, obsession, heroism, comradeship, parental love, and the highest form of love, which is a Christlike sacrifice of self for the good of others. Before he becomes capable of the latter, however, he must struggle against the shadow that haunts him. He calls it "my demon shadow", a presence that masquerades as his very self yet seems to have a life of its own. It follows him throughout his many adventures, always seeking to "disenchant" the world of *Faërie,* making all things meaningless, empty, and unlovely. Through a series of surprising twists of plot, stories within stories, poems, battles, consolations, desolations, songs, successes, and failures, MacDonald draws the reader into a level of consciousness that is close to the flow of dreams. But this is not merely a directionless stream of subconsciousness, for when the reader enters this mysterious world, he is being guided by a master who knows precisely what he is doing and where he is leading us.

Even so, this is early MacDonald, and the lavish details and dramas of his "sub-creation" are not as carefully drawn as those of his extraordinary later book *Lilith.* In the latter (written thirty-seven years after *Phantastes*), the level of insight has grown to the quality of rare wisdom, the perceptions of a virtuous, richly gifted man in old age. It has the added advantage of being, as our children would say, "a terrific story". It is somewhat ornate and challenges the mind of young and old alike with startling imagery and many puzzles, but it is very rewarding. It underlines again and again the choices that men must make between good and evil and the confusion they can experience in knowing which is which. Mr. Vane, the central character, must learn that beneath his heroism, his fine sentiments, and his presumptions there lies a secret pride. Because he lacks wisdom and humility, his efforts to defeat evil often bring about different kinds of evil. He repeatedly discovers that no lasting virtue is possible until he faces his own willfulness and dies to himself. Central to the story is the effort of Adam and Eve and a beautiful woman named Mara, the Lady of Sorrows, to vanquish "the Shadow" (a personification of Satan) and to win the demonically controlled (and controlling) Lilith back to the principles that God the Father wrote into all creation. Lilith clings fiercely to her sovereign self and her power, for she believes that these very things are life itself. Adam, Eve, and Mara try to convince her of the truth: These things are killing her and perpetuating the realm of darkness. She must let go of all power and permit herself to undergo death. Only then will she truly live. Compare this to recent efforts by neopagan "theologians" to popularize the unconverted Lilith (a character who in Jewish folklore is variously called a demon and Adam's first wife), who pursues power and the triumph of the sovereign self as the path to self-divinization—an example of the degeneration into paganism occurring in our times. Wherever one finds figures of evil elevated to heroic status, one should recognize a relentless struggle to win over the mind of the young. One can almost hear the "thrum, thrum" of mesmerizing music.

The present revival of MacDonald's books in Christian circles is a fitting testimony to the quality of his contribution to Christian

literature. Parents who wish to introduce their children to Mac-
Donald should probably begin with his more traditional fairy
tales, such as *The Princess and Curdie, The Princess and the Goblin,
At the Back of the North Wind,* and *The Golden Key.* In the latter
tale, however, there is a curious departure from traditional symbolism that has much to tell us: the two central characters are
trying to find a stairway that will take them to Paradise. They are
instructed to "follow the serpent", a small snake that guides them
to the stairway. If MacDonald intended any symbolic meaning in
this, it may be only to say that the presence of sin and temptation in the world is a sign that we are in a spiritual battle zone
and that even what is fallen can bear a kind of witness to the
light—not unlike the bronze serpent raised up on the staff of
Moses. Or it may be simply that, like many English and Scottish
romantic writers of the last century, he had a fondness for all
creatures, especially the unpopular ones, and wished to "baptize"
even the image of the serpent and thereby restore it to the
original harmony that existed before the fall. While his use of
this symbol is a surprise, perhaps it is nothing more than a re-
minder that no writer has perfect vision, and even the best should
be read with a vigilant eye.

It is some reassurance to note that MacDonald, who published
The Golden Key in 1867, went on to write *At the Back of the
North Wind,* which was published in 1871. It appears that his
sense of the right use of symbols was continually developing and,
indeed, was steering ever more surely on the lines of traditional
cosmology, without losing any of its freshness and originality. In
North Wind the central character, a little boy named Diamond,
searches for a lost poem that had been read to him by his mother
when he was sick and feverish. He does not find the lost poem
but instead comes across another, titled "Little Boy Blue". It is
about a boy who loses his way in the woods and who at first
likes his lostness better than his home. He meets animals, birds,

shadows, wind, a stream, and a snake and calls them to follow him in his wanderings. When he realizes that he does not know what to do with them, he tries to send them away. They protest that they did not follow him for nothing and that he must give them something to do or they will continue to follow him.

> "Oh dear! and oh dear!" with sob and with sigh,
>   Said Little Boy Blue, and began to cry.
>   But before he got far he thought of a thing:
>   And up he stood and spoke like a king.
> "Why do you hustle and jostle and bother?
>   Off with you all! Take me back to my mother."

The elements of nature come up with all sorts of protests and excuses. In reply the boy tells them:

> "Never you mind," said Little Boy Blue;
> "That's what I tell you. If that you won't do,
>   I'll get up at once and go home without you.
>   I think I will; I begin to doubt you."[13]

At this point the snake rises up with a hiss and blocks him. Little Boy Blue hits the snake with his drumstick, steps on its head, kills it, and then goes home with all the other elements of nature passively accompanying him. MacDonald is imparting some subtle insights here: The snake remains inconspicuous as just one of several elements of nature until the boy tries to resist the momentum of his lostness. When the snake manifests itself in a more classical serpent fashion, threatens him, and receives a blow from the stick, it falls down "as if he were dead". But that is not enough, because the serpent is a deceiver. The little king must crush its head. When the serpent is destroyed, the rest of nature joyously submits.

---

[13] *At the Back of the North Wind* (New York: Children's Classics, Crown, 1990), pp. 174–80.

Despite his admiration for MacDonald, Lewis never confers infallibility upon him. *The Great Divorce*, Lewis' fictionalized meditation on damnation and salvation, describes an imaginary bus excursion to the borders of Paradise. There the riders must choose between Heaven and Hell. The conversations that the author overhears between Spirits and Ghosts provide the material of a rebuttal to Blake's famous poem about the "Marriage of Heaven and Hell". Lewis, of course, defends the Christian belief that there never has been, nor could there ever be, such a "marriage". His guide to the borderlands is no less than his hero, George MacDonald, one of the blessed in Paradise (according to the plot line). The entire book is a treatise on MacDonald's warning that "There is no Heaven with a little Hell in it."

There is an important message here, more than the obvious defense of basic Christian theology. MacDonald held some questionable views during his life, such as his belief that animals share the world to come. There is also the problem of his Universalism, the belief that in the end no one will suffer eternal damnation. Indeed, Lewis chides him for this in *The Great Divorce*:

"In your own books, Sir," said I, "you were a Universalist.
You talked as if all men would be saved."

The fictional MacDonald replies at length by refuting the very beliefs that the real MacDonald held on earth. Lewis is attempting to say that MacDonald's errors must surely have come from a great tenderness of heart that was imperfectly balanced by a weak sense of divine justice. He goes on to explain it this way through his characters:

"What some people say on earth is that the final loss of one
soul gives the lie to all the joy of those who are saved."
"Ye see it does not." [says MacDonald]
"I feel in a way that it ought to."

"That sounds very merciful: but see what lurks behind it."

"What?"

"The demand of the loveless and the self-imprisoned that they should be allowed to blackmail the universe: that till they consent to be happy (on their own terms) no one else shall taste joy: that theirs should be the final power; that Hell should be able to veto Heaven. . . . Watch that sophistry or ye'll make a Dog in a Manger the tyrant of the universe."[14]

The Great Divorce was first published in 1946, the same year in which *George MacDonald: An Anthology* was published, a collection prepared by C. S. Lewis and containing the preface in which Lewis described MacDonald's influence upon his own path to Christian faith.[15] Clearly, Lewis saw no contradiction in praising his mentor's positive achievements, on the one hand, and pointing out his shortcomings, on the other. He recognized in his hero a great Christian heart, but one flawed by an incomplete understanding of the nature of evil, of spiritual warfare, of the battle that is waged in creation and, most relentlessly, in human souls. MacDonald was a kindly man raised in a harsh century still reeling from the effects of the shattering of Christendom. The dominant religion of his native culture tended toward a merciless, cold view of human destiny and of God. The doctrine of predestination was in the atmosphere, and MacDonald fled from its ice to the opposite extreme, the illusory warmth of Universalism. Lewis suggests that when this man entered eternal life, his love and his faith were weighed in the balance and found

---

[14] *The Great Divorce* (New York: Macmillan, 1946), p. 124.

[15] The preface has been reprinted as an introduction to the 1981 paperback edition of *Phantastes*, published by Wm. B. Eerdmans Publishing, Grand Rapids, Mich.

to be of more import than his flaws and that in Heaven he was led to perfect truth.

Lewis, MacDonald, and Tolkien are Christian writers whose works are built upon a common moral foundation. They have different strengths and weaknesses, differing styles and emphasis, and varying degrees of explicitness and implicitness with which they express elements of the Christian faith. Tolkien, for example, is the most implicit, for while there is no mention of religion in *The Lord of the Rings*, the trilogy radiates moral consciousness and the splendor of truth. MacDonald's *Lilith* is more explicit, for biblical characters play key roles, and conversion and submission to God are central themes—though in a broad Judeo-Christian context. Lewis' *Narnia* tales and the "space trilogy" are the most explicit, for they are unreservedly centered on Christ and redemption. Each of these authors labors in a different part of the vineyard, and each fulfills a task that is irreplaceable. If Lewis represents those Christian writers whose witness value is most obvious—who labor at the evangelical harvest of souls—Tolkien represents those who prepare the soil, and MacDonald represents those who plant it. Ultimately, Tolkien, Lewis, and Mac-Donald are each concerned with the destiny of human souls. Their primary concerns are salvation, grace, virtue, and spiritual warfare. If at times we are uncertain about how they have used various symbols, this can be turned to the good, for it can stimulate fruitful discussions with our children.

"Are there other universes?" we might ask our young reader (or he might ask us).

"Could God make centaurs if he wanted to?"

"Is magic always bad?"

"Do angels have bodies?"

"Does every planet really have a 'god'?"

"Are there dogs in Heaven?"

"Are Merlin's special powers good or evil?"

"Why didn't Weston see that goodness is better than evil?"

"Is it right to kill wicked people?"

"Why did God use good people to fight evil? Did he have to do it that way?"

"Is good stronger than evil?"

"Why does the devil hate us? Why does he want to control everything?"

And so forth. Hard questions, sometimes unanswerable questions. But if you want your children to grow up to be thinking people, here is a golden opportunity to enrich that process. Genuine literature stimulates the asking. It is not primarily about the implanting of praiseworthy ideas, though of course that is one of its roles. Most of all it is about the imparting of the great adventure, the majesty and mystery of the moral cosmos.

Conclusion

Are Christians Intolerant?

Christmas is approaching as I write the final passages of this book. The stores are full of the very merchandise that these lines have examined. The malls are packed with shoppers. They are, like me, trying to beat the Christmas rush or tap into the pre-Christmas sales, or maybe just get into the spirit of things early. You may have noticed that life in the twentieth century is somewhat tense, and who can be blamed for rushing the season of peace just a little. There's a holiday feeling in the air: the potted pines and the shop windows are all decked out; the robot Santas and the synthetic jingle on the loudspeakers are jolly in about equal portions. As is usual at this time of year, people are more patient with one another, will allow complete strangers to enter elevators before them, will overlook the irritating behavior of the occasional aggressive bargain hunter, and will smile more easily at mothers with small, noisy children. It is the season of tolerance.

Perhaps, then, it would not hurt to be reminded that the Incarnation was, in fact, an act of colossal intolerance on the part of God, by which I mean to say that it was an act of immeasurable love. He loved us so much that he would not let us die in our sins. He was intolerant of our slavery and was born among us for the express purpose of doing something rather drastic about it.

I realize that to use the word *intolerance* is a risky business, for it cannot help but conjure up visions of religious and racial hatreds or the specter of grim moralizers judging their neighbors (and who has not felt the sting of those tongues?). Moreover, it may well be asked if such a tainted word can be properly used to describe a characteristic of God. He is, after all, rich in mercy and slow to anger. But it must be remembered that both the Old and New Testaments speak of times when the justice of God must act—for he will not permit evil to devour everything.

The early Christians were not squeamish about political incorrectness. They knew firsthand that sin meant death to the inner and the exterior life of man. Most of them were converts from paganism, for their world was almost entirely pagan. They had known the effects of falsehood at work in their own minds, hearts, and flesh. They knew that they had been rescued by God's intolerance of their bondage. They exulted in the glorious, shattering good news that Christ was real. He was not a mere theological abstraction or just another deity in an idol-crowded world. He was the one true God, and he was life! That awareness has waned in our era, partly because most people no longer feel endangered by the world of evil, by the possibility of personal slavery to invisible forces or servility to their own fallen natures. Nor do they consider for a moment that a totally paganized society might one day reinstitute an external form of slavery (though, no doubt, it would call it by a more attractive name). But we must understand the lateness of the hour and the urgency of the crisis. My parents' generation struggled with a culture that was losing its spiritual sense; my generation had to struggle with a despiritualized world, and our children must now struggle with a radically dehumanized one. A society that systematically destroys millions of its children through abortion, and in which so many young people take their own lives and take each other's lives is already far gone. Modern man is struggling under a cloud of despair that "spreads and spreads". He has lost the mystery and wonder of being that the eye of childhood knows so well. He has been cheated of the real adventure. He has not known joy. He is now cut loose to stagger about his landscape, his apparently "real" world, in search of his own lost face. Because it is impossible to sustain this unbearable world view for long, he must flee from it into the distractions of sexual immorality, distorted fantasy, the macabre, violence—and, in the worse cases, into cultic religion.

A society sliding back into paganism may try to reassure itself that it is in no worse condition than a society crawling out of paganism. Like two travellers going in opposite directions on a road, for a brief moment they share in passing a common point. But the end of the road for each is very different. The convert from paganism has known darkness and has turned toward the light. Our society has known the light and is turning back toward darkness. This is the crucial difference. It is into the core of this difference that we must speak if we wish to re-evangelize the world.

Travellers from the realm of darkness state loudly and clearly that the land which the lapsed or lapsing Christian is travelling toward is in fact a land of death and degradation. They have been there. They know. When they tell us that few leave that land, that none finds happiness there, and that it is a world of shifting illusory images, they can sound, yes, intolerant. But this intolerance is the intolerance of the physician who has seen an epidemic ravage a people. He is prejudiced against deadly viruses. This is the intolerance of a mother who fiercely protects her little ones from predators. She suffers from a bias against rattlesnakes and wolves. This apparent narrowness is the wisdom of those who have known many roads and have found only one sure route out of the regions of desolation. What such pilgrims have to tell us can sound hard. But their word is true. The Christian's task is now to rediscover a firm commitment to this truth and to show how it can be combined with an effective love of our neighbor.

It goes without saying (although in these confused times it may need repeating) that the urgent need for truth does not mandate us to go rushing about, tearing into our neighbor or our enemy, delivering harsh lectures to this or that erring soul. In the true Christian meaning of the word *charity*, we are to love the personhood of each and every individual human being. This does not mean, however, that we should remain paralyzed and silent regarding acts and ideas that are killing us (and are killing the perpetrators as well). That is not Christian charity. We have a right and a duty to speak the truth with simplicity and calmness, clearly and fearlessly, without rancor or personal condemnation, wherever untruth invades the life of our family.

If modern man is starved for love, he is equally starved for truth. Would it be too much of an exaggeration to say that almost everyone is infected to a degree by the atmospheric lie? The remedy, of course, is exactly what it has always been: Open the doors of our hearts to Jesus Christ, live the Gospels without compromise, love the Church, which is the Mystical Body of Christ, and pray for the flowering of love and the renewal of truth within our communities, churches, families, and oneself—yes, especially oneself.

If I had to choose an image to sum up our times, I would not choose from among the usual ones, such as the Nuclear Age, the Technological Society, the Age of Anxiety, the Computer Generation, the Affluent Society, or the Space Era. I would call it the Age of Noise. In the entire history of mankind, there has never been such a continuous battering of the human brain. The ever-present background throb of machinery, the roar of traffic, the high-pitched buzz of fluorescent lights and computers, *Musak* in elevators and supermarkets, herds of joggers wearing Walkmans, a gaggle of talk shows. A world drowning in chatter! Words, words, words! A thousand voices competing for our attention every day: the communications media, junk mail, candidates for political office, telephone solicitations, and so on and so on . . . the long, sustained roar (and sometimes screech) of our century. Exterior noise and interior noise. The clamor of our anxieties and our skirmishes with the seven deadly sins and a host of lesser evils. The endless inner debates we conduct against real or imagined enemies; and the sweet, rotten allure of the soap operas of the fallen imagination. And of course there is the voice of the accuser, whispering in our ears about our sins and faults. We turn quickly away from that voice, unable to endure more feelings of guilt in an already guilt-ridden society—a society that tells us (again through the media) that Christians are abusers, backward, judgmental, patriarchal, overpopulating, and a menace to the ecology.

Burdened with such an array of exterior and interior pressures, we can find it extremely difficult to face the objective guilt of our fallen natures and open ourselves to the saving power of Jesus Christ. Yet the mere thought of resisting the power of an entire culture with our own strength is utterly exhausting. Overwhelmed, we can be deluded into choosing a less demanding form of faith, a seemingly more "compassionate" kind of religion. We can become the creatures of a powerful conditioning mechanism and, like well-fed slaves, accept a sort of comfortable bondage as our lot in life. We can gradually come to think that the torrent of noise is normal. And when the pressures become intolerable, we might even begin to agree with what the noise is saying.

Saint Paul writes in Romans 12:2: "Do not be conformed to this world but be transformed by the renewal of your mind, that you may prove what is the will of God, what is good and acceptable and perfect." But how can the mind be renewed if it is continually reeling under a bombardment of false words and images? The mind is not renewed simply by packing more and more into it; rather it is renewed by grace and by habits of discernment and by a sincere search for what is good and beautiful and true. Silence is the natural habitat of truth. Prayer is the dwelling place of right seeing. That is why we must reduce the noise in our lives and open the ears of the heart to real listening. We parents especially need moments of complete stillness. We must take great care to make these moments for ourselves and for each other and for our children. We cannot assume that we will be immune to the massive apostasy that is taking place in the Western world. Never in human history has there been such a wholesale loss of faith, nor one that has come about with such startling speed. Much of its momentum is due to the unprecedented power of television, film, and video—of the image—to recreate our understanding of the very shape of reality. Thus, large numbers of Christians simply do not realize that they are apostacizing, and still larger numbers do not understand that they are being prepared mentally to follow. This is the power of impressionism; it is also "peer pressure" on a colossal scale. How very difficult it is to resist an entire culture, and especially for children to do so, because it is a right and good thing for children to grow into awareness of being members of a broader community. They need culture in order to grow properly. It is one of their primary means of learning what it is to be a fully human person in a community of fellow human beings. That is why the solution will never be simply a matter of criticizing the false culture surrounding us. The absolutely essential task of parents is to give their children a true culture, a sure foundation on which to stand.

Suggested Reading

Carlson, Jill. *What Are Your Children Reading? An Alarming Trend in Today's Teen Literature.* Brentwood, Tenn.: Wolgemuth & Hyatt, 1991. [I recommend this book for its well-documented survey of the general situation in children's fiction. Especially helpful is the chapter on parental strategies, "What You Can Do".]

Carpenter, Humphrey. *The Inklings: C. S. Lewis, J. R. R. Tolkien, Charles Williams and Their Friends.* London: Unwin, 1981.

Chandler, Russell. *Understanding the New Age.* Dallas: Word Publishing, 1988.

Hitchcock, James. *What Is Secular Humanism?* Ann Arbor, Mich.: Servant Books, 1982.

Hunt, Gladys. *Honey for a Child's Heart: The Imaginative Use of Books in Family Life.* Grand Rapids, Mich.: Zondervan Books, 1989. [Generally reliable but with some reservations, as with Wilson's book, noted below. Hunt recommends L'Engle, Le Guin, and other questionable authors.]

Kilpatrick, Dr. William. *Books That Build Character.* New York: Simon & Schuster, 1994. [This book is valuable chiefly for its essays by Dr. Kilpatrick. The booklists at the end of the volume were not compiled by the author and contain recommendations for novels by L'Engle, Le Guin, and other questionable authors.]

———. *Psychological Seduction.* Nashville, Tenn.: Thomas Nelson, 1983.

Lewis, C. S. *Of This and Other Worlds.* London: William Collins Co., 1984.

Medved, Michael. *Hollywood vs. America.* New York: HarperCollins, 1992.

Smith, Dr. Wolfgang. *Cosmos and Transcendence.* Peru, Ill.: Sherwood Sugden Publishers, 1984. [See the chapter "The Deification of the Subconscious".]

Tolkien, J. R. R. *Letters.* Boston: Houghton Mifflin, 1981.

———. *The Silmarillion.* Boston: Houghton Mifflin, 1977.

———. *Tree and Leaf.* London: Unwin, 1975. [Cf. the essay "On Fairy Stories".]

Vitz, Paul. *Evidence of Bias in Our Children's Textbooks.* Ann Arbor, Mich.: Servant Books, 1986.

———. *Psychology as Religion: The Cult of Self-Worship.* Grand Rapids, Mich.: Eerdmans, 1985.

Wilson, Elizabeth. *Books Children Love: A Guide to the Best Children's Literature.* Westchester, Ill.: Crossway Books, 1987. [This is a more or less reliable guide to literature for children and young adults, but I recommend it with some reservations. For example, Wilson sees no problem in Madeleine L'Engle's fantasy novels.]

Recommended Family Reading

Compiled by the editorial staff of Bethlehem Books

The following list of over one thousand titles is broken up into five major sections: picture books, easy readers, short chapter books, books for intermediate to young adults, and adult books suitable for older teens. Many books in the upper divisions are appropriate for reading out loud to younger ages. The authors are listed alphabetically in each section. The titles are listed alphabetically under each author (or illustrator), except when there is a series. In the latter case, titles are usually given in chronological order.

Note to parents: This list has come out of twenty years experience with children's books and has been carefully selected to include titles that present themes in conformity with the Judeo-Christian world view. We do not take responsibility for the contents of the books we suggest insofar as individual philosophies of childrearing are concerned; nor do we wish this list to be taken as "the last word". Parents are the final judge as to whether a certain book is appropriate for a particular child or whether it enhances the family's goals and beliefs. We hope you find the list useful and enjoy the books as much as we have.

The following are used throughout the list:

C—winner of the *Caldecott Medal*, annual award in the U.S. for the most distinguished picture book

CH—*Caldecott Medal Honor* book, finalist for the Caldecott Medal

NM—winner of the *Newbery Medal*, annual award in the U.S. for the most distinguished children's title

NH—*Newbery Medal Honor* book, finalist for the Newbery Medal Award

KGM—winner of the *Kate Greenaway Medal*, annual award in the United Kingdom for the most distinguished picture book

KGC—*Kate Greenaway Medal Commendation*, finalist for the Kate Greenaway Medal

CM—winner of the *Carnegie Medal*, annual award in the United Kingdom for the most distinguished children's title

CMH—*Carnegie Medal Honor* book, finalist for the Carnegie Medal

*—books recently or still in print.

PICTURE BOOKS

Editions of older classic picture books written and/or illustrated by such pioneer artists in the field of children's literature as L. Leslie Brooke, Randolph Caldecott, Walter Crane, Kate Greenaway, Arthur Rackham, and Jessie Willcox Smith are not listed but should not be overlooked. Librarians will know of recent, available editions. At the end of this section is a short fairy tale and fantastical story list.

Ardizzone, Edward (author and illustrator)
    The Tim and Ginger series:
        Little Tim and the Brave Sea Captain
      * *Tim All Alone*, KGM
      * *Tim and Charlotte*
      * *Tim and Ginger*
        Tim in Danger
        Tim to the Lighthouse
      * *Tim's Friend Towser*
        Ship's Cook Ginger
        Tim and Lucy Go to Sea
        Tim's Last Voyage

Arnold, Mary
    * *The Fussy Angel*, illus. by **Patsy Nealon**

Arnosky, Jim (author and illustrator)
    * *All Night Near the Water*
    * *Come Out, Muskrats*
    * *Crinkleroot's Guide to Knowing the Trees*
    * *Crinkleroot's Guide to Walking in Wild Places*
    * *Crinkleroot's Twenty-Five Birds Every Child Should Know*
    * *Crinkleroot's Twenty-Five Mammals Every Child Should Know*
    * *Raccoons and Ripe Corn*
    * *Watching Foxes*
    and many more . . .

Artzybasheff, Boris (author and illustrator)
  Seven Simeons, CH

Barklem, Jill (author and illustrator)
  * *Brambly Autumn Book*
  The Brambly Hedge Birthday Book
  * *Brambly Spring Book*
  * *Brambly Summer Book*
  * *Brambly Winter Book*
  The Secret Staircase

Baynes, Pauline (author and illustrator)
  * *Bilbo's Last Song* (written by **J. R. R. Tolkien**)
  * *The Puffin Book of Nursery Rhymes* (ed. by **Peter** and **Iona Opie**)
  Snail and Caterpillar (written by **Helen Piers**), KGC
  The Song of the Three Holy Children
  * *Thanks Be to God: Prayers from around the World*

Beskow, Elsa (author and illustrator)
  * *Around the Year*
  Children of the Forest
  * *The Flowers' Festival*
  * *Ollie's Ski Trip*
  * *Pelle's New Suit*
  * *Peter in Blueberry Land*
  * *Peter's Old House*
  The Tale of the Little, Little Old Woman
  Woody Hazel and Little Pip

Bishop, Claire Huchet
  * *The Five Chinese Brothers*, illus. by **Kurt Wiese**
  The Man Who Lost His Head, illus. by **Robert McCloskey**
  Twenty-Two Bears, illus. by **Kurt Wiese**

Blades, Ann (author and illustrator)
  * *A Boy of Tache*

A Candle for Christmas (written by **Jean Speare**)
* *Mary of Mile 18*
A Salmon for Simon (written by **Betty Waterton**)

Brown, Margaret Wise

* *A Child's Goodnight Book*, illus. by **Jean Charlot**, CH
* *Goodnight Moon*, illus. by **Clement Hurd**
* *The Little Fir Tree*, illus. by **Barbara Cooney**
* *Little Fur Family*, illus. by **Garth Williams**
  The Little Island, illus. by **Leonard Weisgard** (under the pseudonym of **Golden MacDonald**), C
  The Noisy Book, illus. by **Leonard Weisgard**
* *The Runaway Bunny*, illus. by **Clement Hurd**
* *Wheel on the Chimney*, illus. by **Tibor Gergely**, CH

Brown, Michael

  Shackleton's Epic Voyage, illus. by **Raymond Briggs**

Burkert, Nancy Ekholm (illustrator)

* *The Fir Tree* (written by **Hans Christian Andersen**)
* *The Nightingale* (written by **Hans Christian Andersen**)
* *Snow White and the Seven Dwarves* (written by **Jacob** and **Wilhelm Grimm**)

Burton, Virginia Lee (author and illustrator)

* *Calico the Wonder Horse: Or, the Saga of Stewy Stinker*
* *Choo Choo: The Story of the Little Engine Who Ran Away*
* *Katie and the Big Snow*
* *The Little House*, C
* *Maybelle, the Cable Car*
* *Mike Mulligan and His Steam Shovel*

Clark, Ann Nolan

  Along Sandy Trails, photos by **Alfred A. Cohn**
  The Desert People, illus. by **Allan Houser**
* *In My Mother's House*, illus. by **Velino Herrera**, CH
  A Santo for Pasqualita, illus. by **Mary Villarejo**
* *There Still Are Buffalo*, illus. by **A. Standing Soldier**

Cole, Joanna
>> *A Gift from St. Francis: The First Crèche*, illus. by **Michéle Lemieux**

Collington, Peter (author and illustrator)
>> * *A Small Miracle*

Cooney, Barbara (author and illustrator)
>> * *American Folk Songs for Children* (written by **Ruth Seeger**)
>> * *American Folk Songs for Christmas* (written by **Ruth Seeger**)
>> * *Chanticleer and the Fox* (written by **Geoffrey Chaucer**), C
>> *A Garland of Games and Other Diversions: An Alphabet Book*
>> * *Island Boy*
>> *The Little Juggler*
>> *A Little Prayer* (old French prayer)
>> * *Miss Rumphius*
>> * *The Owl and the Pussy-Cat* (written by **Edward Lear**)
>> * *The Ox-Cart Man* (written by **Donald Hall**), C
>> * *The Remarkable Christmas of the Cobbler's Sons* (written by **Ruth Sawyer**)
>> * *Seven Little Rabbits* (written by **John Becker**)
>> * *Snow White and Rose Red* (written by **Jakob** and **Wilhelm Grimm**)
>> * *The Story of Christmas*

D'Aulaire, Ingri and **Edgar Parin** (authors and illustrators)
>> * *Abraham Lincoln*, C
>> * *Benjamin Franklin*
>> * *D'Aulaires' Book of Greek Myths*
>> * *D'Aulaires' Norse Gods and Giants*
>> *Buffalo Bill*
>> *Children of the Northlights*
>> * *Columbus*
>> * *George Washington*
>> * *Leif the Lucky*
>> *Pocahontas*

De Paola, Tomie (author and illustrator)
>> *Christopher: The Holy Giant*

* *The Cloud Book*
* *The Clown of God*
* *Francis, the Poor Man of Assisi*
* *The Lady of Guadalupe*
   The Little Friar Who Flew (written by **Patricia Lee Gauch**)
   Mary, the Mother of Jesus
* *The Miracles of Jesus*
* *Nana Upstairs and Nana Downstairs*
* *The Quicksand Book*
* *The Parables of Jesus*
* *Patrick, Patron Saint of Ireland*
* *Petook: An Easter Story* (written by **Caryll Houselander**)
* *The Popcorn Book*

Dupasquier, Philippe (author and illustrator)
   Andy's Pirate Ship
   Dear Daddy
   Going West
* *The Great Escape*
* *No More Television!*
   The Busy Day series:
* *Busy Day at the Airport*
* *Busy Day at the Building Site*
* *Busy Day at the Factory*
* *Busy Day at the Garage*
* *Busy Day at the Harbor*
* *Busy Day at the Train Station*

Duvoisin, Roger (author and illustrator)
* *Petunia*, plus six other *Petunia* books
* *White Snow, Bright Snow* (written by **Alvin Tresselt**), C
   The Happy Lion series (written by **Louise Fatio**):
   The Happy Lion
   The Happy Lion and the Bear
   The Happy Lion Roars
   The Happy Lion's Quest
   The Three Happy Lions

Ets, Marie Hall (author and illustrator)
* * *In the Forest*, CH
* * *Just Me*, CH
* *Mister Penny's Race Horse*, CH
* *Mr. T. W. Anthony Woo: The Story of a Cat and a Dog and a Mouse*, CH
* * *Nine Days to Christmas*, C
* * *Play with Me*, CH

Fisher, Aileen
* * *The Story of Easter*, illus. by **Stefano Vitale**

Flack, Marjorie (author and illustrator)
* * *Angus and the Cat*
* * *Angus and the Ducks*
* * *Angus Lost*
* * *Ask Mr. Bear*
* * *Boats on the River*, illus. by **Jay Barnum**, CH
* * *The Story about Ping* (with **Kurt Wiese**)

Freeman, Don (author and illustrator)
* *Add-a-Line Alphabet*
* * *Corduroy*
* * *Dandelion*
* *Fly High, Fly Low*, CH
* * *Norman the Doorman*
* * *A Pocket for Corduroy*
* *Will's Quill*

Fritz, Jean
* * *Brendan, the Navigator*, illus. by **Enrico Arno**
* *The Man Who Loved Books*, illus. by **Trina Schart Hyman**

Gag, Wanda (author and illustrator)
* *ABC Bunny*
* * *The Funny Thing*
* * *Millions of Cats*

Gibbons, Gail (author and illustrator)
  * *Beacons of Light: Lighthouses*
  * *Check It Out! A Book about Libraries*
  * *From Path to Highway: The Story of the Boston Post Road*
  * *The Great St. Lawrence Seaway*
    Knights in Shining Armor
  * *The Puffins Are Back!*
    and many more . . .

Gilman, Phoebe (author and illustrator)
  * *Something from Nothing*

Godden, Rumer
  * *Four Dolls* (collection of four short books), illus. by **Pauline Baynes**
    The Mouse House, illus. by **Adrienne Adams**
    St. Jerome and the Lion, illus. by **Jean Primrose**

Goudey, Alice
    The Day We Saw the Sun Come Up, illus. by **Adrienne Adams**, CH
    The Good Rain, illus. by **Nora Unwin**
    Houses from the Sea, illus. by **Adrienne Adams**, CH
    Red Legs, illus. by **Marie Nonnast**

Graham, Lorenz
    David He No Fear, illus. by **Ann Grifalconi**
  * *Every Man Heart Lay Down*, illus. by **Colleen Browning**
    God Wash the World and Start Again, illus. by
      Clare Romano Ross
    Hongry Catch the Foolish Boy, illus. by **James Brown, Jr.**

Gramatky, Hardie (author and illustrator)
    Creeper's Jeep
    Hercules: The Story of an Old-Fashioned Fire Engine
    Homer and the Circus Train
  * *Little Toot*
    Little Toot on the Grand Canal
    Little Toot on the Mississippi

Little Toot on the Thames
Little Toot through the Golden Gate
Loopy
Sparky: The Story of a Little Trolley Car

Hoban, Russell

* *Bedtime for Frances*, illus. by **Garth Williams**
* *Best Friends for Frances*, illus. by **Lillian Hoban**
* *A Birthday for Frances*, illus. by **Lillian Hoban**
* *Bread and Jam for Frances*, illus. by **Lillian Hoban**

Hodges, Margaret

* *Brother Francis and the Friendly Beasts*, illus. by **Ted Lewin**
* *The Kitchen Knight*, illus. by **Trina Schart Hyman**
* *Saint George and the Dragon*, illus. by **Trina Schart Hyman**, C
  St. Jerome and the Lion, illus. by **Barry Moser**
* *Saint Patrick and the Peddler*, illus. by **Paul Brett**
  Silent Night: The Song and Its Story, illus. by **Tim Ladwig**
* *The Wave*, illus. by **Blair Lent**, CH

Hurd, Thacher (author and illustrator)

* *Mystery on the Docks*

Jones, Elizabeth Orton (illustrator)

Small Rain: Verses from the Bible (selected by **Jessie Orton Jones**), CH
* *Prayer for a Child* (written by **Rachel Field**), C

Kahl, Virginia (author and illustrator)

The Baron's Booty
The Duchess Bakes a Cake
The Habits of Rabbits
Plum Pudding for Christmas

Krahn, Fernando (author and illustrator)

Amanda and the Mysterious Carpet
Arthur's Adventures in the Abandoned House
Catch That Cat!
The Mystery of the Giant's Footprints

The Secret in the Dungeon
Who's Seen the Scissors?

Kurelek, William (author and illustrator)
Picture books of interest for older children:
* * *Lumberjack*
* * *A Northern Nativity*
* * *A Prairie Boy's Summer*
* * *A Prairie Boy's Winter*

Lawson, Robert (author and illustrator)
* * *They Were Strong and Good*, C

Leaf, Munro
* * *The Story of Ferdinand*, illus. by **Robert Lawson**

Lenski, Lois (author and illustrator)
* * *The Big Book of Mr. Small*
* *Cowboy Small*
* *The Little Airplane*
* *The Little Auto*
* *The Little Farm*
* *The Little Sailboat*
* *Policeman Small*

Lindgren, Astrid
Illustrated by **Ilon Wikland**:
* * *Christmas in Noisy Village*
* * *I Don't Want to Go to Bed*
* * *I Want a Brother or Sister*
* *I Want to Go to School, Too*
* *The Runaway Sleigh Ride*
* *Springtime in Noisy Village*
Illustrated by **Harald Wiberg**:
* *Christmas in the Stable*
* * *The Tomten*
* * *The Tomten and the Fox*

Lindgren, Barbro
Illustrated by **Eva Eriksson**:
* * *Sam's Ball*
* * *Sam's Bath*
* * *Sam's Car*
* * *Sam's Cookie*
* * *Sam's Teddy Bear*
* * *Sam's Wagon*

Lindman, Maj (author and illustrator)
* * The Flicka, Ricka, Dicka series
* * The Snipp, Snapp, Snurr series

McCloskey, Robert (author and illustrator)
* * *Blueberries for Sal*, CH
* * *Burt Dow, Deep Water Man*
* * *Journey Cake, Ho!* (written by **Ruth Sawyer**), CH
* * *Lentil*
* * *Make Way for Ducklings*
* * *One Morning in Maine*, CH
* * *Time of Wonder*, C

McCully, Emily Arnold (author and illustrator)
  The Christmas Gift
* * *First Snow*
* * *Mirette on the High Wire*, C
* * *Picnic*
* * *School*

Merrill, Jean
  Shan's Lucky Knife, illus. by **Ronni Solbert**
  Tell about the Cowbarn, Daddy, illus. by **Lili Wronker**

Miller, Edna (author and illustrator)
  Mousekin Finds a Friend
  Mousekin's ABC
* * *Mousekin's Close Call*
  Mousekin's Easter Basket
* * *Mousekin's Fables*

     * *Mousekin's Family*
     Mousekin's Golden House
     Mousekin's Lost Woodland
     Mousekin's Mystery
     Mousekin's Thanksgiving
     Mousekin's Woodland Birthday
     Mousekin's Woodland Sleepers
     Mousekin Takes a Trip
     Pebbles: A Packrat

Milne, A. A.
    Illustrations by **E. H. Shepard**:
     * *The House at Pooh Corner*
     * *Now We Are Six*
     * *When We Were Very Young*
     * *Winnie-the-Pooh*

O'Brien, Michael (author and illustrator)
     * *The Small Angel*

Owens, Mary Beth (author and illustrator)
     * *A Caribou Alphabet*
     * *Counting Cranes*

Oxenbury, Helen (author and illustrator)
     * *The Quangle Wangle's Hat* (written by **Edward Lear**), KGM
     The Queen and Rosie Randall
    Series:
     Macmillan Big Board Books
     * Out and About Books
     * Oxenbury Board Books
     * Tom and Pippo Books

Parkin, Rex (author and illustrator)
     The Red Carpet

Paton Walsh, Jill
     Lost and Found, illus. by **Mary Rayner**

Petersham, Miska and **Maud** (authors and illustrators)
    An American ABC, CH
   * *The Box with Red Wheels*
    The Christ Child
    The Circus Baby
    Joseph and His Brothers
    Moses
   * *The Rooster Crows: A Book of American Rhymes and Jingles*, C
   * *The Story of David*
   * *The Story of Ruth*

Pickthall, Marjorie
    The Worker in Sandalwood, illus. by **Frances Tyrrell**

Pochocki, Ethel
   * *A Penny for a Hundred*, illus. by **Mary Beth Owens**
    Rosebud and Red Flannel, illus. by **Mary Beth Owens**

Politi, Leo (author and illustrator)
    A Boat for Peppe
    The Butterflies Come
    Juanita, CH
    Little Leo
    The Mission Bell
    Moy Moy
    Pedro, the Angel of Olivera Street, CH
    Piccolo's Prank
    Rosa
    Saint Francis and His Animals
   * *Song of the Swallows*, C
   * *Three Stalks of Corn*

Potter, Beatrix (author and illustrator)
   * *The Tale of Benjamin Bunny*
   * *The Tale of Jemima Puddle-Duck*
   * *The Tale of Mrs. Tiggy-Winkle*
   * *The Tale of Peter Rabbit*
   * *The Tale of the Pie and the Patty-Pan*
   * *The Tale of Squirrel Nutkin*

    * *The Tale of Two Bad Mice*
    and others . . .

Price, Christine (author and illustrator)
    One Is God: Two Old Counting Songs
    The Valiant Chattee-Maker

Provensen, Alice and **Martin** (authors and illustrators)
    * *The Glorious Flight across the Channel with Louis Bleriot, C*
    The Mother Goose Book
    * *Our Animal Friends at Maple Hill Farm*
    * *An Owl and Three Pussycats*
    * *Peaceable Kingdom*
    Shaker Lane
    * *Town and Country*
    The Year at Maple Hill Farm

Reid, Barbara (author and illustrator)
    The New Baby Calf
    * *Two by Two*

Scarry, Richard (author and illustrator)
    Richard Scarry's Best Word Book Ever
    Richard Scarry's Cars and Trucks and Things that Go
    Richard Scarry's Postman Pig and His Busy Neighbors
    and many more . . .

Selsam, Millicent
    * *Backyard Insects*
    * *How Kittens Grow*
    * *How Puppies Grow*
    * *How to be a Nature Detective*, illus. by **Ezra Jack Keats**

Smucker, Barbara
    * *Selina and the Bear Paw Quilt*, illus. by **Janet Wilson**

Spier, Peter (author and illustrator)
    Bored, Nothing to Do
    * *Crash! Bang! Boom!*

 The Erie Canal
* *The Fox Went Out on a Chilly Night: An Old Song*, CH
* *London Bridge Is Falling Down*
* *Noah's Ark*, C
 Oh, Were They Ever Happy
* *People*
* *Peter Spier's Christmas*
* *Peter Spier's Circus*
* *Peter Spier's Rain*
* *The Star-Spangled Banner*
 Tin Lizzie
* *We the People: The Story of the U.S. Constitution*

Steig, William (author and illustrator)
* *Amos and Boris*
* *Brave Irene*, CM
* *Yellow and Pink*

Taylor, Mark
 Illustrated by **Graham Booth**:
  The Case of the Purloined Compass
  Henry the Castaway
  Henry the Explorer
  Henry Explores the Jungle
  Henry Explores the Mountains

Tripp, Wallace (compiler and illustrator)
* *Granfa' Grig Had a Pig and Other Rhymes without Reason from Mother Goose*
* *A Great Big Ugly Man Came Up and Tied His Horse to Me: A Book of Nonsense Verse*
* *Marguerite, Go Wash Your Feet!*

Tudor, Tasha (author and illustrator)
 Child's Garden of Verses (written by **Robert L. Stevenson**)
* *First Graces*
* *First Prayers*
* *Give Us This Day Our Daily Bread: The Lord's Prayer*
* *The Lord Is My Shepherd: The Twenty-Third Psalm*

* *Mother Goose*, CH
  The Night before Christmas (written by **Clement C. Moore**)
* *One Is One*, CH

Turkle, Brinton (author and illustrator)
    The Adventures of Obadiah
  * *Deep in the Forest*
    Obadiah the Bold
  * *Rachel and Obadiah*
  * *Thy Friend, Obadiah*, CH

Turner, Ann (author and illustrator)
  * *Apple Valley Year*
  * *The Christmas House*
  * *Dakota Dugout*
  * *Dust for Dinner*
  * *Katie's Trunk*

Van Stockum, Hilda (author and illustrator)
  * *The Angels' Alphabet*
  * *A Day on Skates: A Story of a Dutch Picnic*, NH
    Kersti and Saint Nicholas
    Little Old Bear
    Patsy and the Pup

Ventura, Piero (author and illustrator)
  * *Clothing: Garments, Styles and Uses*
  * *Great Composers*
    Great Painters
    Man and the Horse
    Michelangelo's World
    The Painter's Trick
    Piero Ventura's Book of Cities
    There Once Was a Time

Watts, Bernadette (author and illustrator)
    Varenka

Whelan, Gloria
>   * *Bringing the Farmhouse Home*, illus. by **Jada Rowland**
>   * *The Miracle of Saint Nicholas*, illus. by **Judith Brown**
>   *A Week of Racoons*, illus. by **Lynn Musinger**

Wojciechowski, Susan
>   * *The Christmas Miracle of Jonathan Toomey*, illus. by **P. J. Lynch**

Yashima, Taro (author and illustrator)
>   * *Crow Boy*, CH
>   *Momo's Kitten*
>   * *Umbrella*, CH
>   *Youngest One*

FAIRY, ANCIENT, AND FANTASTICAL TALES

Aesop
>   *Aesop's Fables*, ed. and illus. by **Boris Artzybasheff**
>   *Fables*, illus. by **Arthur Rackham**

Andersen, Hans Christian
>   * *The Complete Fairy Tales and Stories*

Asbjornsen, Peter, and **Jorgen E. Moe**
>   *East o' the Sun and West o' the Moon*,
>   trans. by **George W. Dasent**

Browne, Frances
>   *Granny's Wonderful Chair*

Carroll, Lewis
>   * *Alice's Adventures in Wonderland*
>   * *Through the Looking-Glass*

Coatsworth, Elizabeth
>   * *The Cat Who Went to Heaven*, illus. by **Lynd Ward**, NM

Collodi, Carlo
>*Pinocchio*, illus. by **Roberto Innocenti**

Colum, Padraic
>*The Arabian Nights: Tales of Wonder and Magnificence*, ed.,
>illus. by **Lynd Ward**
>*The Big Tree of Bunlahy: Stories of My Own Countryside*,
>illus. by **Jack B. Yeats**, NH
>* *The Children's Homer: The Adventures of Odysseus and the Tale of
>Troy*, illus. by **Willy Pogany**
>*The Children of Odin: The Book of Northern Myths*,
>illus. by **Willy Pogany**
>* *The Golden Fleece and the Heroes Who Lived before Achilles*,
>illus. by **Willy Pogany**, NH
>* *Orpheus: Myths of the World*, illus. by **Boris Artzybasheff**
>*The Voyagers, Being Legends and Romances of Atlantic Discovery*,
>illus. by **Wilfred Jones**, NH

Coolidge, Olivia
>* *Caesar's Gallic War*
>*Egyptian Adventures*, illus. by **Joseph Low**
>* *Greek Myths*, illus. by **Edouard Sandoz**
>*Legends of the North*, illus. by **Edouard Sandoz**
>* *Lives of Famous Romans*
>* *The Trojan War*, illus. by **Edouard Sandoz**

Dickens, Charles
>*A Christmas Carol*, illus. by **Roberto Innocenti**

Finger, Charles
>*Tales from the Silver Lands*, illus. by **Paul Honoré**, NM

Green, Roger Lancelyn
>* *King Arthur and His Knights of the Round Table*
>* *Myths of the Norsemen*
>* *Tales of Ancient Egypt*
>* *Tale of Troy*
>* *Tales of the Greek Heroes*

Grimm, Jacob and **Wilhelm Grimm** (editors)

>   *The Fairy Tales of the Brothers Grimm*, illus. by **Arthur
>   Rackham**
>   *Sixty Fairy Tales of the Brothers Grimm*, illus. by **Arthur
>   Rackham**
>   various other eds., illus. by **Walter Crane** and **George
>   Cruikshank**

Hawthorne, Nathaniel

>   * *Tanglewood Tales: Being a Second Wonder-Book*
>   * *The Wonder-Book for Boys and Girls*

Innocenti, Roberto (illustrator)

>   *A Christmas Carol* (written by **Charles Dickens**)
>   *Pinocchio* (written by **Carlo Collodi**)

Lagerlof, Selma

>   * *The Wonderful Adventures of Nils*

Lang, Andrew (editor)

>   * *The Blue Fairy Book* and eleven other volumes,
>   illus. by **H. J. Ford**

Lear, Edward

>   * *The Complete Nonsense of Edward Lear*

MacDonald, George

>   * *At the Back of the North Wind*
>   * *The Gifts of the Child Christ*
>   * *The Princess and Curdie*
>   * *The Princess and the Goblin*

Olenius, Elsa (editor)

>   *Great Swedish Fairy Tales*, illus. by **John Bauer**,
>   trans. by **Holger Lundbergh**

Perrault, Charles

>   *Tales of Mother Goose*

Pyle, Howard (author and illustrator)

 * *The Story of King Arthur and His Knights*

 * *The Wonder Clock: Four-and-Twenty Marvelous Tales, One for*
  Each Hour of the Day

Ruskin, John

 * *The King of the Golden River,* illus. by **Richard Doyle**

Serraillier, Ian

 * *Beowulf the Warrior,* illus. by **Mark Severin**

EASY READERS

There are numerous "beginning-to-read" series of books to help the novice reader practice his new skill. Here are a sampling of titles to help get started.

Adler, David
* The Cam Jansen mystery series (over fifteen titles)
* *My Dog and the Birthday Mystery*
  My Dog and the Green Sock Mystery
  My Dog and the Knock Knock Mystery
  Redwoods Are the Tallest Trees in the World

Alderson, Sue Ann
  Ida and the Wool Smugglers

Aliki
* *Corn Is Maize: The Gift of the Indians*
* *Digging Up Dinosaurs*
* *I'm Growing!*
* *My Feet*
* *My Five Senses*
* *My Hands*
  and others . . .

Benchley, Nathaniel
* *George the Drummer Boy*
* *Oscar Otter*
* *Red Fox and His Canoe*
  Running Owl the Hunter
* *Sam the Minuteman*
* *Small Wolf*
* *Snorri and the Strangers*

Bishop, Claire Huchet
> *Georgette*
> *The Truffle Pig*

Byars, Betsy
> * *The Golly Sisters Go West*
> * *The Golly Sisters Ride Again*
> * *Hooray for the Golly Sisters*

Gage, Wilson
> *The Crow and Mrs. Gaddy*
> *Down in the Boondocks*
> *Mrs. Gaddy and the Fast-Growing Vine*
> * *My Stars, It's Mrs. Gaddy*

Hoff, Syd
> * *Albert the Albatross*
> * *Barkley*
> * *Barney's Horse*
> * *Captain Cat*
> * *Chester*
> * *Danny and the Dinosaur*
> *Gentleman Jim and the Great John L.*
> * *The Horse in Harry's Room*
> * *Julius*
> * *Mrs. Brice's Mice*
> * *Sammy the Seal*
> and others . . .

Hurd, Edith Thacher
> * *Come and Have Fun*
> * *Johnny Lion's Bad Day*
> * *Johnny Lion's Book*
> *Johnny Lion's Rubber Boots*
> * *Starfish*
> *Stop Stop*

Kessler, Leonard
> * *Here Comes the Strikeout*

      * *Kick, Pass and Run*
      * *Last One in Is a Rotten Egg*
        On Your Mark, Get Set, Go!

Kumin, Maxine W., and Anne Sexton
      Eggs of Things
      More Eggs of Things

Lobel, Arnold
      * *Days with Frog and Toad*
      * *Frog and Toad All Year*
      * *Frog and Toad Are Friends*, NH
      * *Frog and Toad Together*
        and others . . .

Lopshire, Robert
      How to Make Snop Snappers and Other Fine Things

Lowrey, Janette S.
      Six Silver Spoons

McCully, Emily Arnold
      * *The Grandma Mix-up*
      * *Grandmas at Bat*
      * *Grandmas at the Lake*

Minarik, Else Holmelund
      * *Cat and Dog*
      * *Father Bear Comes Home*
      * *Little Bear*
      * *Little Bear's Friend*
      * *Little Bear's Visit*
      * *A Kiss for Little Bear*
      * *No Fighting, No Biting!*

Mitchell, Barbara
      Cornstalks and Cannonballs
      * *Hush Puppies*
        Tomahawks and Trombones

Parish, Peggy
* *Amelia Bedelia*
* *Amelia Bedelia and the Baby*
* *Amelia Bedelia and the Surprise Shower*
* *Amelia Bedelia Goes Camping*
* *Amelia Bedelia Helps Out*
  Be Ready at Eight
* *Come Back, Amelia Bedelia*
* *Good Work, Amelia Bedelia*
* *Merry Christmas, Amelia Bedelia*
  Mr. Adam's Mistake
* *Play Ball, Amelia Bedelia*
* *Teach Us, Amelia Bedelia*
* *Thank You, Amelia Bedelia*
* *Too Many Rabbits*
  and others . . .

Quackenbush, Robert
* The Detective Mole series
* The Henry series (five titles)
* The Humorous Biography series (nineteen titles)
* The Miss Mallard mystery series (fifteen titles)
  The Pete Packrat and Sally Gopher series
  The Piet Potter series (six titles)
* The Sherlock Chick series (four titles)

Roop, Peter and Connie
* *Buttons for General Washington*
* *Keep the Lights Burning, Abbie*

Sandin, Joan
* *The Long Way to a New Land*
* *The Long Way Westward*

Selsam, Millicent
* *Egg to Chick*
* *Greg's Microscope*
  More Potatoes!
  Seeds and More Seeds

Sharmat, Marjorie W.
    * The Nate the Great mystery series (over 15 titles)

Van Woerkom, Dorothy O.
    Abu Ali: Three Tales of the Middle East
    Becky and the Bear
    The Friends of Abu Ali: Three More Tales of the Middle East
    Meat Pies and Sausages
    Sea Frog, City Frog
    Tit for Tat

Yolen, Jane
    * The Commander Toad series

SHORT CHAPTER BOOKS

The reading level of the following titles varies from book to book. Generally, the books are shorter, with more illustration and with a lower beginning age interest (roughly, ages seven to nine) than the longer ones listed in the Intermediate Books section. All are suitable for reading aloud to a younger child; many make excellent family read-alouds.

Almedingen, E. M.
One Little Fir Tree: A Christmas Carol of a Finnish Landscape, illus. by **Denise Brown**

Anderson, C. W. (author and illustrator)
A Filly for Joan
High Courage
The Horse of Hurricane Hill
Salute
The Blaze series:
* *Billy and Blaze: A Boy and His Pony*
Blaze and the Gypsies
* *Blaze and the Forest Fire*
Blaze Finds the Trail
* *Blaze and Thunderbolt*
* *Blaze and the Mountain Lion*
Blaze and the Indian Cave
* *Blaze and the Lost Quarry*
Blaze and the Gray Spotted Pony
Blaze Finds the Forgotten Roads
* *Blaze Shows the Way*

Bishop, Claire Huchet
All Alone, illus. by **Feodor Rojankovsky**
Pancakes-Paris, illus. by **Georges Schreiber**
* *Twenty and Ten*, illus. by **William Pene du Bois**

Bulla, Clyde Robert

Excellent resource for the beginning readers:

Illustrated by **Grace Paull**:

A Ranch for Danny

Riding the Pony Express

* *The Secret Valley*

Star of Wild Horse Canyon

Surprise for a Cowboy

Illustrated by other artists:

Benito, illus. by **Valenti Angelo**

* *Daniel's Duck*, illus. by **Joan Sandin**

Dexter, illus. by **Glo Coalson**

* *Eagle Feather*, illus. by **Tom Two Arrows**

* *Ghost Town Treasure*, illus. by **Don Freeman**

John Billington, Friend of Squanto, illus. by **Peter Burchard**

* *Pirate's Promise*, illus. by **Peter Burchard**

St. Valentine's Day, illus. by **Valenti Angelo**

Song of St. Francis, illus. by **Valenti Angelo**

* *Squanto, Friend of the Pilgrims*, illus. by **Peter Burchard**

Stories of Favorite Operas, illus. by **Robert Galster**

Viking Adventure, illus. by **Douglas Gorsline**

Burchard, Peter (author and illustrator)

Short, high interest novels for ages 10 and up:

Charlotte Forten: A Black Teacher in the Civil War

Jed: The Story of a Yankee Soldier and a Southern Boy

Rat Hell: A Story of Escape (Civil War)

Carlson, Natalie Savage

Chalou, illus. by **Julian Willett**

* *The Family under the Bridge*, illus. by **Garth Williams**, NH

Jean Claude's Island, illus. by **Nancy Ekholm Burkert**

The Letter on the Tree, illus. by **John Kaufmann**

Sailor's Choice, illus. by **George Loh**

School Bell in the Valley, illus. by **Gilbert Riswold**

The Orpheline series:

The Happy Orpheline, illus. by **Garth Williams**

A Brother for the Orphelines, illus. by **Garth Williams**

A Pet for the Orphelines, illus. by **Fermin Rocker**

The Orphelines in the Enchanted Castle, illus. by **Adriana Saviozzi**

A Grandmother for the Orphelines, illus. by **David White**

Catherall, Arthur

Of interest for a wide age range:

Duel in the High Hills (U.S. edition not illustrated)

Kidnapped by Accident, illus. by **Victor Ambrus**

Lapland Outlaw (various illustrators)

Last Horse on the Sands, illus. by **David Farris**

Prisoners in the Snow, illus. by **Victor Ambrus**

The Strange Intruder (U.S. edition not illustrated)

Caudill, Rebecca

* *The Best-Loved Doll*, illus. by **Elliott Gilbert**

* *A Certain Small Shepherd*, illus. by **William Pene du Bois**

* *Did You Carry the Flag Today, Charley?*,
   illus. by **Nancy Grossman**

* *A Pocketful of Cricket*, illus. by **Evaline Ness**, CH

The Bonnie series, illus. by **Decie Merwin**:

Happy Little Family

Schoolhouse in the Woods

Up and Down the River

Schoolhouse in the Parlor

Coatsworth, Elizabeth

The Cave, illus. by **Alan Houser**

George and Red, illus. by **Paul Giovanopoulos**

The Hand of Apollo, illus. by **Robin Jacques**

Jock's Island, illus. by **Lilian Obligado**

Jon the Unlucky, illus. by **Esta Nesbitt**

The Littlest House, illus. by **Marguerite Davis**

The Noble Doll, illus. by **Leo Politi**

The Sally series, illus. by **Helen Sewell**:

Away Goes Sally

The Fair American

Five Bushel Farm

The White Horse

The Wonderful Day

The American Adventures history series (for newer readers):
  First Adventure (1620–1650), illus. by **Ralph Ray**
  The Wishing Pear (1650–1700), illus. by **Ralph Ray**
  Boston Bells (1700–1750), illus. by **Manning Lee**
  Aunt Flora (1750–1800), illus. by **Manning Lee**
  Old Whirlwind (1800–1850), illus. by **Manning Lee**
  The Sod House (1850–1900), illus. by **Manning Lee**
  Cherry Ann (1900–1945), illus. by **Manning Lee**

Colver, Anne
  Bread and Butter Indian, illus. by **Garth Williams**

Dalgliesh, Alice
  Adam and the Golden Cock, illus. by **Leonard Weisgard**
  * *The Bears on Hemlock Mountain*, illus. by **Helen Sewell**, NH
  The Columbus Story, illus. by **Leo Politi**
  * *The Courage of Sarah Noble*, illus. by **Leonard Weisgard**, NH
  * *The Thanksgiving Story*, illus. by **Helen Sewell**, CH

Daly, Maureen
  The Ginger Horse, illus. by **Wesley Dennis**
  The Small War of Sergeant Donkey, illus. by **Wesley Dennis**

De Angeli, Marguerite (author and illustrator)
  Book of Nursery and Mother Goose Rhymes, CH
  Bright April (African American)
  * *Copper-toed Boots*
  * *The Door in the Wall: Story of Medieval London*, NM
  Elin's Amerika (Swedish pioneers)
  Henner's Lydia (Amish)
  Jared's Island (1760s, Colonial America)
  * *The Lion in the Box*
  Petite Suzanne (French Canadian)
  Skippack School
  Thee, Hannah! (Quaker)
  Turkey for Christmas
  Up the Hill (Polish American)
  Whistle for the Crossing
  * *Yonie Wondernose* (Amish), CH

Dillon, Eilis
Illustrated by **Richard Kennedy**:
The Key
The Lion Cub
The Road to Dunmore
Under the Orange Grove

Freedman, Florence B.
True account, of interest to older children as well:
* *Two Tickets to Freedom: The True Story of Ellen and William Craft, Fugitive Slaves*

Fritz, Jean
* *And Then What Happened, Paul Revere?*, illus. by **Margot Tomes**
* *The Cabin Faced West*, illus. by **Feodor Rojankovsky**
* *Can't You Make Them Behave, King George?*, illus. by **Tomie de Paola**
* *George Washington's Breakfast*, illus. by **Paul Galdone**
* *Make Way for Sam Houston!*, illus. by **Elise Primavera**
* *Shh! We're Writing the Constitution*, illus. by **Tomie de Paola**
* *What's the Big Idea, Ben Franklin?*, illus. by **Margot Tomes**
* *Where Was Patrick Henry on the 29th of May?*, illus. by **Margot Tomes**
* *Who's That Stepping on Plymouth Rock?*, illus. by **J. B. Handelsman**
* *Why Don't You Get a Horse, Sam Adams?*, illus. by **Trina Schart Hyman**
* *Will You Sign Here, John Hancock?*, illus. by **Trina Schart Hyman**
and others . . .

Godden, Rumer
* *Great Grandfather's House*, illus. by **Valerie Littlewood**
The Mouse Wife, various illustrators
* *The Rocking Horse Secret*, illus. by **Juliet S. Smith**
Illustrated by **Adrienne Adams**:
Candy Floss
* *The Fairy Doll*

Impunity Jane: The Story of a Pocket Doll
* *The Story of Holly and Ivy*

Goudey, Alice E.
Danny Boy, illus. by **Paul Brown**
Jupiter and the Cats, illus. by **Paul Brown**
Sunnyvale Fair, illus. by **Paul Galdone**
Illustrated by **Garry MacKenzie**:
Here Come the Bears!
Here Come the Beavers!
Here Come the Bees!
Here Come the Deer!
Here Come the Dolphins!
Here Come the Elephants!
Here Come the Lions!
Here Come the Raccoons!
Here Come the Seals!
Here Come the Whales!
Here Come the Wild Dogs!

Graham, Robin Lee, with **Derek Gill**
The Boy Who Sailed around the World Alone

Hautzig, Esther
* *A Gift for Mama*, illus. by **Donna Diamond**

Hays, Wilma Pitchford
Abe Lincoln's Birthday, illus. by **Peter Burchard**
Christmas on the Mayflower, illus. by **Leonard Weisgard**
Eli Whitney and the Machine Age, illus. by **Alfred Petersen**
George Washington's Birthdays, illus. by **Peter Burchard**
Pilgrim Thanksgiving, illus. by **Leonard Weisgard**
Samuel Morse and the Telegraph, illus. by **Richard Mayhew**
The Scarlet Badge, illus. by **Peter Burchard**
The Story of Valentine, illus. by **Leonard Weisgard**

Heiderstadt, Dorothy
A Bow for Turtle, illus. by **William Ferguson**

Indian Friends and Foes, illus. by **David Humphreys Miller**
Marie Tanglehair, illus. by **Ursula Koering**
More Indian Friends and Foes, illus. by **David Humphreys Miller**

Hoff, Carol
* *Johnny Texas*, illus. by **Bob Meyers**
* *Johnny Texas on the San Antonio Road*, illus. by **Earl Sherwan**
* *Wilderness Pioneer: Stephen F. Austin*, illus. by **Robert Todd**

Holling, Holling C. (author and illustrator)
* *Minn of the Mississippi*
* *Paddle-to-the-Sea*
* *Pagoo*
* *Seabird*
* *Tree in the Trail*

Lexau, Joan M.
Archimedes Takes a Bath, illus. by **Salvatore Murdocca**

Lindgren, Astrid
* *The Children of Noisy Village*, illus. by **Ilon Wikland**
The Children on Troublemaker Street, illus. by **Ilon Wikland**
Happy Times in Noisy Village, illus. by **Ilon Wikland**

McLaughlin, Lorrie
The Trouble with Jamie, illus. by **Lewis Parker**
West to the Cariboo, illus. by **Joe Rosenthal**
(Other books in this Buckskin Books series: *The Scout Who Led an Army*, by **Lareine Ballantyne**; *The Heroine of Long Point*, by **Leslie** and **Lois Benham**; *Adventure at the Mill*, by **Barbara** and **Heather Bramwell**; *The Man with Yellow Eyes*, by **Catherine Clark**; *The Great Canoe* and *Lukey Paul from Labrador*, by **Adelaide Leitch**; *Father Gabriel's Cloak*, by **Beulah Garland Swayze**; *Danger in the Coves*, by **Frances C. Thompson**; *Escape from Grand Pre*, by **Frances C. Thompson**; *The Boy and the Buffalo*, by **Kerry Wood**; *Andrew Tolliver*, by **Richard Wright**.)

Mason, Miriam
>*Caroline and Her Kettle Named Maud*, illus. by **Kathleen Voute**
>*Caroline and the Seven Little Words*, illus. by **Paul Frame**
>*A Pony Called Lightning*, illus. by **C. W. Anderson**
>*Susannah: The Pioneer Cow*, illus. by **Maud** and **Miska**
>   **Petersham**

Merrill, Jean
>*Maria's House*, illus. by **Frances Gruse Scott**
>*The Superlative Horse: A Tale of Ancient China*,
>   illus. by **Ronni Solbert**

Monjo, Ferdinand N.
>* *The Drinking Gourd*, illus. by **Fred Brenner** (Underground
>   Railroad)

Perkins, Lucy Fitch (author and illustrator)
>The following are a sampling of the twenty-six original titles of
>*Twins of the World:*
>>*The Cave Twins*
>>* *The Dutch Twins*
>>*The Japanese Twins*
>>*The Norwegian Twins*
>>* *The Pioneer Twins*
>>*The Spartan Twins*
>>*The Swiss Twins*

Pochocki, Ethel
>*Grandma Bagley Leads the Way*, illus. by **Sarah Mohler**
>*Grandma Bagley to the Rescue*, illus. by **Sarah Mohler**
>* *More Once upon a Time Saints*, illus. by **Kathy Holbrook**
>* *Once upon a Time Saints*, illus. by **Tom Matt**
>* *One-of-a-Kind Friends: Saints and Heroes for Kids*,
>   illus. by **Mary Beth Owens**
>* *The Wind Harp and Other Angel Stories*,
>   illus. by **Mary Beth Owens**

Shemin, Margaretha
>* *The Little Riders*, illus. by **Peter Spier**

Steele, William
Humorous tall tales:
Andy Jackson's Water Well, illus. by **Michael Ramus**
Daniel Boone's Echo, illus. by **Nicolas Mordvinoff**
Davy Crockett's Earthquake, illus. by **Nicolas Mordvinoff**
Historical fiction illustrated by **Paul Galdone**:
* * *The Buffalo Knife*
* *The Far Frontier*
* * *Flaming Arrows*
* *The Lone Hunt*
* * *The Perilous Road*, NH
* *Tomahawks and Trouble*
* *Wilderness Journey*
* * *Winter Danger*
Historical fiction illustrated by **Charles Beck**:
Trail through Danger
The Year of the Bloody Sevens

Stuart, Jesse
Illustrated by **Robert G. Henneberger**:
* * *The Beatinest Boy*
* * *A Penny's Worth of Character*
* * *Red Mule*

Syme, Ronald
The following titles are a mix of shorter biographies and longer ones for children 10 and up:
African Traveler: The Story of Mary Kingsley,
illus. by **Jacqueline Tomes**
Nigerian Pioneer: The Story of Mary Slessor,
illus. by **Jacqueline Tomes**
Illustrated by **William Stobbs**:
Alexander Mackenzie: Canadian Explorer
Balboa: Finder of the Pacific
Captain Cook: Pacific Explorer
Cartier: Finder of the St. Lawrence
Champlain of the St. Lawrence
Cortes of Mexico
De Soto: Finder of the Mississippi

First Man to Cross America: The Story of Cabeza de Vaca
Francis Drake: Sailor of the the Unknown Seas
Francisco Pizarro: Finder of Peru
Henry Hudson
John Smith of Virginia
La Salle of the Mississippi
Magellan: First around the World
The Man Who Discovered the Amazon
On Foot to the Arctic: The Story of Samuel Hearne
Sir Henry Morgan Buccaneer
Vasco da Gama: Sailor toward the Sunrise
Walter Raleigh

Thompson, Mary Wolfe
Two in the Wilderness
Wilderness Wedding
Wilderness Winter

Tobias, Tobi
Marian Anderson, illus. by **Symeon Shimin**
Maria Tallchief, illus. by **Michael Hampshire**

Van Stockum, Hilda (author and illustrator)
Gerrit and the Organ, illus. by the author
King Oberon's Forest, illus. by **Brigid Marlin**
Mogo's Flute, illus. by **Robin Jacques**

Whelan, Gloria
Friends, illus. by **Jenifer Thomas**
* *Hannah*, illus. by **Leslie Bowman**
* *The Indian School*, illus. by **Gabriela Dellosso**
* *Next Spring an Oriole*, illus. by **Pamela Johnson**
* *Night of the Full Moon*, illus. by **Leslie Bowman** (sequel to
    Next Spring an Oriole)
* *The Shadow of the Wolf*, illus. by **Tony Meers**
* *Silver*, illus. by **Stephen Marchesi**

Wuorio, Eva-Lis
Illustrated by **Edward Ardizzone**:
The Island of Fish in the Trees (a Balearic island)
Kali and the Golden Mirror (Aegean island of Skyros)
The Land of Right Up and Down (country of Andorra)
The Singing Canoe (Canadian wilderness)

Yates, Elizabeth
 * *Carolina's Courage*
 * *Sarah Whitcher's Story*

BOOKS FOR INTERMEDIATE READERS

The following books cover a wide age range. The suggested reading level is listed with each author. Some of the titles are given with a brief word or two about their setting. At the end of the list is a short section mentioning series by more than one author.

Aldrich, Thomas Bailey
For ages 10 and up:
* *The Story of a Bad Boy*

Allen, Merritt Parmelee
For ages 10 and up:
    Battle Lanterns (American Revolution)
    East of Astoria (founding of Astoria, Oregon)
    The Flicker's Feather (American Revolution)
    Johnny Reb (Civil War)
    Make Way for the Brave: The Oregon Quest (Oregon Trail)
    and others . . .

Almedingen, E. M.
For ages 12 and up:
    Anna (18th-century Moscow)
    Ellen
    Fanny (19th century)
    Katia (19th century)
    Young Mark (18th century)

Anckarsvard, Karin
For ages 10 and up:
    Doctor's Boy
    The Riddle of the Ring
    Struggle at Soltuna (sequel to *Doctor's Boy*)
The Aunt Vinnie series:
    Aunt Vinnie's Invasion

Aunt Vinnie's Victorious Six
The Nordvik mystery series:
  The Mysterious Schoolmaster
  The Robber Ghost
  The Madcap Mystery

Angelo, Valenti (author and illustrator)
For ages 9 and up:
  Bells of Bleecker Street (New York, World War II)
  The Hill of Little Miracles
  The Honey Boat
  The Marble Fountain (Italy, post–World War II)
  The Merry Marcos
  Paradise Valley
  The Tale of a Donkey
The Nino series:
  Nino, NH
  * *The Golden Gate*
  The Rooster Club

Annixter, Paul and Jane
For ages 12 and up:
  Buffalo Chief
  The Runner
  Swift Water
  Wagon Scout (post-Civil War)
  Windigo

Armstrong, William H.
For ages 14 and up:
  Barefoot in the Grass: The Story of Grandma Moses
  The Education of Abraham Lincoln
The Sounder trilogy:
  * *Sounder*, NM
  * *The Sour Land*
  The Macleod Place

Atwater, Richard and Florence
For ages 9 and up:
* *Mr. Popper's Penguins*, NH

Bailey, Carolyn Sherwin
For ages 9 and up:
Flickertail
Finnegan II: His Nine Lives
* *Miss Hickory*, NM

Balderson, Margaret
For ages 12 and up:
When Jays Fly to Bárbmo

Barrie, J. M.
For ages 11 and up:
* *Peter and Wendy*

Bawden, Nina
For ages 10 and up:
Carrie's War
The House of Secrets
Three on the Run

Bell, Gertrude
For ages 11 and up:
Posse of Two (pre–Civil War Missouri/Kansas border conflicts)

Benary-Isbert, Margot
For ages 12 and up:
* *The Ark*
Castle at the Border
* *Dangerous Spring*
The Long Way Home
* *Rowan Farm* (sequel to *The Ark*)
* *Under a Changing Moon*

Bendick, Jeanne (author and illustrator)
For ages 10 and up:
  * *Archimedes and the Door of Science*

Bianco, Margery Williams
For ages 9 to 12:
  Bright Morning
  Poor Cecco
For ages 12 and up:
  Winterbound, NH

Bill, Alfred H.
For ages 12 and up:
  The Clutch of the Corsican: A Tale of the Days of the Downfall of the Great Napoleon
  The Red Prior's Legacy: The Story of the Adventures of an American Boy in the French Revolution

Boden, Hilda
For ages 7 to 12:
  Faraway Farm
  Foxes in the Valley
  The House by the Sea
  Marlows at Castle Cliff
  Marlows at Newgate
  Marlows Win a Prize
  Water Wheel, Turn!

Bonham, Frank
For ages 12 and up:
  Burma Rifles: A Story of Merrill's Marauders (World War II)
  Devilhorn
  The Ghost Front (Battle of the Bulge)
  War beneath the Sea (World War II)

Bothwell, Jean
For ages 10 and up:
  The Boat Boy
  The Dancing Princess

>   *The Emerald Clue*
>   *The Missing Violin*
>   *The Promise of the Rose*
>   *The Red Scarf*
>   *Ride, Zarina, Ride*
>   *Ring of Fate*
>   *Romany Girl*
>   *Search for the Golden Bird* (sequel to *The Thirteenth Stone*)
>   *The Silver Mango Tree*
>   *Sword of a Warrior*
>   *The Thirteenth Stone*
>   *White Fawn of Phalera*

Brady, Charles A.

For ages 9 to 14:
>   *The King's Thane* (7th-century Northumbria)
>   *Sword of Clontarf* (11th-century Ireland)

Brill, Ethel C.

For ages 9 and up:
>   * *Madeleine Takes Command* (New France, 1692)

Brink, Carol Ryrie

For ages 9 and up:
>   *Andy Buckram's Tin Men*
>   * *Baby Island*
>   * *Caddie Woodlawn*, NM
>   *Family Grandstand*
>   *Family Sabbatical* (sequel to *Family Grandstand*)
>   *Louly*
>   *Mademoiselle Misfortune*
>   * *Magical Melons: More Stories about Caddie Woodlawn*
>   * *The Pink Motel*
>   *Winter Cottage*

Burnford, Sheila

For ages 10 and up:
>   * *The Incredible Journey*

Burton, Hester

For ages 12 and up:
    Castor's Away (Battle of Trafalgar)
    In Spite of All Terror (World War II)
    No Beat of Drum (England/Tasmania, 1829–1831)
    Time of Trial, CM (England, 1801)

Butler, Beverly

For ages 12 and up:
    The Fur Lodge
    Song of the Voyager

Campbell, Marion

For ages 10 and up:
    The Wide Blue Road (1263, Norman, Scottish, and Norse)

Carr, Mary Jane

For ages 10 and up:
    Children of the Covered Wagon (Oregon Trail)
    Young Mac of Fort Vancouver (Hudson Bay Company)

Catherall, Arthur

For ages 10 and up:
    Lone Seal Pup
    Shanghaied!
    Sicilian Mystery
    Ten Fathoms Deep
    Tenderfoot Trapper
    Thunder Dam
    Yugoslav Mystery
    and many others . . .

Caudill, Rebecca

For ages 12 and up:
    Barrie and Daughter (Appalachia)
    The Far-Off Land (1780, Tennessee)
    Tree of Freedom, NH (1780s, Kentucky)

Chrisman, Arthur Bowie
For ages 9 and up:
  * *Shen of the Sea*, NM

Church, Richard
For ages 11 and up:
    Five Boys in a Cave

Clark, Ann Nolan
For ages 8 to 12:
    Little Navajo Bluebird
    Looking-for-Something: The Story of a Stray Burro of Ecuador
    Magic Money
    Paco's Miracle
  * *Secret of the Andes*, NM (Peru)
For ages 10 and up:
    All This Wild Land (Finnish immigrants to America)
    Brother André of Montreal
    Father Kino: Priest to the Pimas
    Hoofprint on the Wind (Ireland)
    Santiago (Guatamala)
    Year Walk (Basques in America)

Clarke, Mary Stetson
For ages 12 and up:
    The Iron Peacock
    Petticoat Rebel

Clarke, Pauline
For ages 10 and up:
  * *The Return of the Twelves*

Cleaver, Vera and Bill
For ages 14 and up:
    Trial Valley (Sequel to *Where the Lilies Bloom*)
  * *Where the Lilies Bloom*

Coatsworth, Elizabeth

For ages 9 and up:
> *Alice-All-by-Herself*
> *Door to the North: A Saga of Fourteenth Century America*
> *The Last Fort: A Story of the French Voyagers*
> *The Sword of the Wilderness* (Colonial America)

Constant, Alberta Wilson

For ages 11 and up:
> *Miss Charity Comes to Stay* (1893, Cherokee Strip Land Run)
> *The Motoring Millers* (sequel to *Those Miller Girls*)
> *Those Miller Girls* (1911, Kansas)

Coolidge, Susan

For ages 11 and up:
> *Clover*
> *In the High Valley*
> * *What Katy Did*
> *What Katy Did at School*
> *What Katy Did Next*

De Angeli, Marguerite (author and illustrator)

For ages 11 and up:
> *The Black Fox of Lorne*, NH

De Jong, Dola

For ages 10 and up:
> *The Level Land* (World War II, Holland)
> *Return to the Level* (sequel to *The Level Land*, post–World War II)

De Jong, Meindert

For ages 9 and up:
> *Bells of the Harbor* (sequel to *Dirk's Dog, Bello*)
> *Dirk's Dog, Bello*
> *Far Out on the Canal*
> * *The House of Sixty Fathers*, NH (China, World War II)
> * *Hurry Home, Candy*, NH

    * *Shadrach*, NH
    * *The Wheel on the School*, NM

De Leeuw, Cateau
For ages 10 and up:
    Determined to Be Free (Revolutionary War)
    Fear in the Forest (18th-century Ohio frontier)
    Where Valor Lies (written with **Adele de Leeuw**) (Crusades)

Dick, Trella Lamson
For ages 8 and up:
    Tornado Jones
    Tornado Jones on Sentinel Mountain
For ages 10 and up:
    Flag in Hiding
    The Island on the Border: A Civil War Story
    Valiant Vanguard

Dillon, Eilís
For ages 9 and up:
    Children of Bach
    The Coriander
    A Family of Foxes
    The Fort of Gold
    The Island of Ghosts
    The Island of Horses
   * *The Lost Island*
    The San Sebastian
   * *The Sea Wall*
    The Seals
    The Seekers
   * *The Singing Cave*

Dodge, Mary Mapes
For ages 11 and up:
   * *Hans Brinker; or, The Silver Skates*

Doman, Regina

For ages 14 and up:
   * *Snow White and Rose Red: A Modern Fairy Tale*

Duncan, Jane

For ages 9 and up:
   Camerons Ahoy!
   Camerons at the Castle
   Camerons Calling
   Camerons on the Hills
   Camerons on the Train

Dygard, Thomas

For ages 10 and up:
   * *Backfield Package*
   * *Forward Pass*
   * *Game Plan*
   * *Halfback Tough*
   * *Infield Hit*
   * *Outside Shooter*
     Point Spread
   * *Quarterback Walk-on*
     Rebound Caper
   * *The Rebounder*
   * *The Rookie Arrives*
   * *Running Scared*
   * *Running Wild*
   * *Soccer Duel*
   * *Tournament Upstart*
   * *Wilderness Peril*
   * *Winning Kicker*

Edmonds, Walter

For ages 9 and up:
   * *The Matchlock Gun*, NM (1750s, New York)

Enright, Elizabeth

For ages 10 and up:
   * *Gone-Away Lake*, NH

　　　Return to Gone-Away (sequel to *Gone-Away Lake*)
　　* *Thimble Summer*, NM
　The Melendy Family series:
　　* *The Saturdays*
　　* *The Four-Story Mistake*
　　* *Then There Were Five*

Erdman, Loula Grace

　For ages 12 and up:
　　The Good Land
　　The Wind Blows Free
　　The Wide Horizon

Estes, Eleanor

　For ages 9 and up:
　　The Alley
　　* *The Hundred Dresses*, NH
　　The Tunnel of Hugsy Goode (sequel to *The Alley*)
　The Moffat series:
　　* *The Moffats*
　　The Middle Moffat, NH
　　Rufus M, NH
　The Pye series:
　　* *Ginger Pye*, NM
　　Pinky Pye

Field, Rachel

　For ages 11 and up:
　　* *Calico Bush*, NH
　　* *Hitty: Her First Hundred Years*, NM

Fife, Dale

　For ages 9 to 14:
　　North of Danger (World War II)

Finger, Charles

　　Courageous Companions (voyage of Magellan)

Finlayson, Ann

For ages 12 and up:

Greenhorn on the Frontier (sequel to *Redcoat in Boston*)

Redcoat in Boston

Fisher, Aileen

For ages 10 to 14:

Cherokee Strip: The Race for Land (1893, Oklahoma Land Run)

Homestead of the Free: The Kansas Story

My Cousin Abe

Timber!: Logging in Michigan

* *Trapped by the Mountain Storm*

Fisher, Dorothy Canfield

For ages 9 and up:

* *Understood Betsy*

Fitzgerald, John D.

For ages 10 and up:

Brave Buffalo Fighter

* *The Great Brain*

* *More Adventures of the Great Brain*

Fleischman, Sid

For ages 9 and up:

* *By the Great Horn Spoon!*

* *Chancy and the Grand Rascal*

* *Humbug Mountain*

* *Mr. Mysterious and Company*

Flory, Jane (author and illustrator)

For ages 9 and up:

Clancy's Glorious Fourth

Faraway Dream

The Golden Venture (California Gold Rush)

One Hundred and Eight Bells

Ramshackle Roost

A Tune for the Towpath

The Amanda Jane series:
  Peddler's Summer
  Mist on the Mountain

Forbes, Esther
  For ages 12 and up:
    * *Johnny Tremain: A Novel for Young and Old*, NM

Ford, Lauren
  For ages 10 and up:
    * *Our Lady's Book*

French, Allen
  For ages 10 and up:
    The Lost Baron
    * *The Red Keep*
    * *The Story of Rolf and the Viking Bow*

Fritz, Jean
  For ages 11 and up:
    * *Brady* (pre–Civil War)
    * *Early Thunder* (Revolutionary War)
    I, Adam (mid-19th century)

Fry, Rosalie (author and illustrator)
  For ages 9 and up:
    The Castle Family
    The Echo Song
    Gypsy Princess
    The Riddle of the Figurehead
    September Island

Fyson, J. G.
  For ages 12 and up:
    The Journey of the Eldest Son (sequel to *The Three Brothers of Ur*)
    The Three Brothers of Ur (time of Abraham)

Garnett, Henry

For ages 9 to 14:
The Blood Red Crescent (1571, Lepanto)
A Trumpet Sounds (16th-century England)

Garthwaite, Marion

For ages 12 and up:
Tomás and the Red Headed Angel (early California)

Gates, Doris

For ages 10 and up:
* *Blue Willow*, NH
The Elderberry Bush
Sensible Kate

George, Jean Craighead

For ages 10 and up:
* *My Side of the Mountain*, NH
* *The Summer of the Falcon*

Gipson, Fred

For ages 12 and up:
Home Place
The Old Yeller series:
* *Old Yeller*, NH
* *Savage Sam*
Little Arliss

Godden, Rumer

For ages 10 and up:
The Diddakoi
* *The Doll's House*
Home Is the Sailor
The Kitchen Madonna
Little Plum
* *Listen to the Nightingale*
Miss Happiness and Miss Flower, CMH
Mr. McFadden's Hallowe'en
Operation Sippacik

Graham, Lorenz
  For ages 12 and up:
  The David Williams series:
    * *South Town*
      North Town
      Whose Town?
      Return to South Town

Gray, Elizabeth Janet (also known as **Elizabeth Gray Vining**)
  For ages 10 and up:
    * *Adam of the Road*, NM (13th century)
      Beppy Marlowe of Charles Town (Colonial Carolinas)
      I Will Adventure (Shakespeare's England)
      Meggy MacIntosh, NH (Colonial Carolinas)
      Penn, NH
      Young Walter Scott, NH

Hámori, László
  For ages 12 and up:
      Dangerous Journey (1950s, Hungary)
      Flight to the Promised Land (1948, Yemenite Jews)

Harnett, Cynthia (author and illustrator)
  For ages 10 and up:
      The Great House (1690, St. Paul's Cathedral)
      The Merchant's Mark, CM (1493, England)
      The Sign of the Green Falcon (1415, London)
      Stars of Fortune (ancestors of George Washington)
      The Writing on the Hearth (1439, Oxford)

Hawes, Charles Boardman
  For ages 12 and up:
    * *The Dark Frigate*, NM (mid-17th century)
      The Great Quest (1826)
      The Mutineers (1860s)

Hays, John
  For ages 11 and up:
      Buckskin Colonist (Selkirk settlers)

Bugles in the Hills (early days of the Mounties)
The Dangerous Cove (settlement of Newfoundland)
Flaming Prairie (Riel Rebellion)
A Land Divided (removal of Acadians)
On Loyalist Trails (loyalists' emigration to Canada)
Quest in the Cariboo (British Columbia gold rush)
Rebels Ride at Night (Mackenzie Rebellion)
The Steel Ribbon (building of Canadian Pacific Railway)
Treason at York (War of 1812)

Heiderstadt, Dorothy

For ages 9 to 12:
Frontier Leaders and Pioneers
Indian Friend and Foes
Marie Tanglehair (1660s, Ursulines in Quebec)
More Indian Friend and Foes

Henry, Marguerite

For ages 9 and up:
Benjamin West and His Cat Grimalkin
* *Justin Morgan Had a Horse*, NH
* *King of the Wind*, NM
* *Misty of Chincoteague*, NH
and many others . . .

Hewes, Agnes Danforth

For ages 10 and up:
Codfish Market, NH
Glory of the Seas, NH (18th-century Boston clipper ships)
Spice and the Devil's Cave, NH (Vasco da Gama)
Spice Ho! A Story of Discovery (nonfiction, Spice Trade)
Swords on the Sea (14th-century Venice)

Hodges, C. Walter (author and illustrator)

For ages 10 and up:
The Marsh King (sequel to *The Namesake*)
The Namesake (King Alfred)

Hodges, Margaret
For ages 11 and up:
The Joshua Cobb series:
The Hatching of Joshua Cobb
The Making of Joshua Cobb
The Freewheeling of Joshua Cobb
The High Riders

Holm, Anne
For ages 12 and up:
* *North to Freedom*

Hubbard, Margaret Ann
For ages 9 to 14:
The Blue Gonfalon (1099, First Crusade)

Hunt, Irene
For ages 12 and up:
* *Across Five Aprils*, NH (Civil War)
* *Up a Road Slowly*, NM

James, Will
For ages 12 and up:
* *Smoky: The Cowhorse*, NM

Jane, Mary C.
For ages 9 to 12:
The Ghost Rock Mystery
Mystery Back of the Mountain
Mystery at Pemaquid Point
Mystery at Shadow Pond
* *Mystery in Old Quebec*
Mystery on Echo Ridge

Jewett, Eleanore
For ages 10 and up:
Big John's Secret (Middle Ages)
Cobbler's Knob

The Hidden Treasure of Glaston, NH (12th century)
Mystery at Boulder Point

Johnson, Gerald

Very readable nonfiction for ages 11 and up:
America Grows Up: A History for Peter
America Is Born: A History for Peter, NH
America Moves Forward: A History for Peter, NH
British Empire: An American View of Its History from 1776 to 1945
The Congress
The Constitution
The Presidency
The Supreme Court

Kaestner, Erich

For ages 10 and up:
Emil and the Detectives

Keith, Harold

For ages 9 and up:
Bluejay Boarders
Runt of Rodgers School
Susy's Scoundrel
* *Will Rogers, A Boy's Life: An Indian Territory Childhood*
For ages 12 and up:
Brief Garland
Komantica
The Obstinate Land
* *Rifles for Watie*, NM

Kelly, Eric

For ages 12 and up:
The Blacksmith of Vilno: A Tale of Poland in the Year 1832
The Golden Star of Halich
* *Trumpeter of Krakow: A Tale of the Fifteenth Century*, NM

Kendall, Carol
For ages 10 and up:
 * *Gammage Cup*, NH
   Whisper of Glocken

Kjelgaard, Jim
For ages 11 and up:
   Boomerang Hunter
   Desert Dog
   Double Challenge
   Hi Jolly! (1850s, camels in the American desert)
   Lion Hound
   Rebel Siege (American Revolution)
 * *Stormy*
   Wolf Brother (1880s, Arizona)
   and others . . .
The Big Red series:
 * *Big Red*
 * *Irish Red, Son of Big Red*
 * *Outlaw Red, Son of Big Red*
The Snow Dog series:
 * *Snow Dog*
 * *Wild Trek*
The Trailing Trouble series:
   A Nose for Trouble
   Trailing Trouble

Knight, Eric
For ages 9 and up:
 * *Lassie Come Home*

Konigsburg, E. L.
For ages 11 and up:
 * *From the Mixed-Up Files of Mrs. Basil E. Frankweiler*, NM

Krumgold, Joseph Quincy
For ages 11 and up:
 * *. . . And Now Miguel*, NM
 * *Onion John*, NM

Lamb, Harold

For ages 14 and up:

  * *Durandal* (Crusades and the Mongols)

    Kirdy: The Road out of the World (17th century, Cossacks)

  * *The Sea of the Ravens* (sequel to *Durandal*)

Lampman, Evelyn

For ages 9 and up:

    The Bounces of Cynthiann' (early Oregon settlement)

    Tree Wagon (Oregon Trail)

For ages 12 and up:

    Bargain Bride (Oregon frontier life)

    Princess of Fort Vancouver (John McLoughlin's daughter)

    The Year of Small Shadow

Latham, Jean Lee

For ages 10 and up:

    Anchor's Aweigh: The Story of David Glasgow Farragut

  * *Carry On, Mr. Bowditch*, NM

    Trail Blazer of the Seas (Lieutenant Matthew Fontaine Maury)

    Young Man in a Hurry (Cyrus Field, transatlantic cable)

Lathrop, West

For ages 11 and up:

    Black River Captive (1757, New Hampshire)

    Keep the Wagons Moving! (1846, Oregon Trail)

    Unwilling Pirate

Lawrence, Ann

For ages 12 and up:

    Between the Forest and the Hills

    The Half-Brothers

Lawson, Robert (author and illustrator)

For ages 9 and up:

  * *Ben and Me: A New and Astonishing Life of Benjamin Franklin, as Written by His Good Mouse, Amos*

  * *Captain Kidd's Cat*

  * *The Fabulous Flight*

    * *The Great Wheel*, NH
    * *Mr. Revere and I*
    * *Rabbit Hill*, NM
       The Tough Winter (sequel to *Rabbit Hill*)

Leighton, Margaret
    For ages 12 and up:
       Journey for a Princess (9th century)

Lenski, Lois (author and illustrator)
    For ages 10 and up:
       Bound Girl of Cobble Hill
    * *Indian Captive: The Story of Mary Jemison*, NH
       Ocean-Born Mary
       Phoebe Fairchild, NH
    * *Strawberry Girl*, NM

Lewis, C. S.
    For ages 7 and up:
    The Chronicles of Narnia series:
    * *The Lion, the Witch and the Wardrobe*
    * *Prince Caspian*
    * *The Voyage of the "Dawn Treader"*
    * *The Silver Chair*
    * *The Horse and His Boy*
    * *The Magician's Nephew*
    * *The Last Battle*

Lewis, Elizabeth Foreman
    For ages 10 and up:
    * *Young Fu of the Upper Yangtze*, NM

Lindquist, Jennie D.
    For ages 9 and up:
    The Nancy series:
       The Golden Name Day, NH
    * *The Little Silver House*
    * *The Crystal Tree*

Locke, Elsie

For ages 12 and up:
The Runaway Settlers

Lofting, Hugh

For ages 9 and up:
 * *The Voyages of Dr. Dolittle*, NM
 and many others . . .

Lomask, Milton

For ages 9 to 14:
Cross among the Tomahawks (New France)
 * *The Curé of Ars: The Priest Who Out-talked the Devil*
 * *Saint Isaac and the Indians*
Ship's Boy with Magellan

Lovelace, Maud Hart

For ages 6 to 11:
The Betsy series:
 * *Betsy-Tacy*
 * *Betsy-Tacy and Tib*
 * *Betsy and Tacy Go Downtown*
 * *Betsy and Tacy over the Big Hill*

Lownsbery, Eloise

For ages 11 and up:
Boy Knight of Reims
A Camel for a Throne

McCloskey, Robert

For ages 9 to 14:
 * *Centerburg Tales*
 * *Homer Price*

McGraw, Eloise Jarvis

For ages 10 and up:
Crown Fire
 * *The Golden Goblet*, NH (Ancient Egypt)
Master Cornhill (Fire of London)

    * *Moccasin Trail*, NH (Oregon Trail settlers)
     The Money Room
    * *Sawdust in His Shoes*
     The Striped Ships (Bayeux Tapestry)
   For ages 12 and up:
    * *Mara, Daughter of the Nile* (Ancient Egypt)

McLean, Allan Campbell

   For ages 12 and up:
    Master of Morgana
    Ribbon of Fire
    A Sound of Trumpets

McMeekin, Isabel McLennan

   For ages 10 and up:
    Journey Cake (18th century, North Carolina/Kentucky)
    Juba's New Moon (sequel to *Journey Cake*)

McSwigan, Marie

   For ages 9 to 14:
    * *Snow Treasure*

Mantle, Winifred

   For ages 11 and up:
   The Westcott and Lester series:
    The Hiding Place
    Tinker's Castle
    The Chateau Holiday
    The Question of the Painted Cave

Meader, Stephen

   For ages 10 and up:
    Away to Sea (1821, slaving)
    The Black Buccaneer (1700s, pirates)
    A Blow for Liberty (American Revolution)
    Boy with a Pack, NH (1837, Erie Canal)
    Buffalo and Beaver (mountain men)
    Cape May Packet (War of 1812)
    Clear for Action!

Down the Big River (frontier, Ohio River)
Everglades Adventure (1870)
The Fish Hawk's Nest (1820s)
Guns for the Saratoga (American Revolution)
Jonathan Goes West
Longshanks (1828, Abe Lincoln)
The Long Trains Roll (World War II)
Lumberjack
Phantom of the Blockade (American Civil War)
T-Model Tommy (early trucking)
Red Horse Hill
The River of Wolves (French and Indian Wars)
Sabre Pilot (Korean War)
The Sea Snake (World War II)
Shadow in the Pines
The Voyage of the Javelin (Yankee Clipper Ships)
Whaler round the Horn (1850s)
Who Rides in the Dark?

Means, Florence Crannell
For ages 12 and up:
    A Candle in the Mist
  * *The Moved-Outers*, NH
    Penny for Luck
    Shadow over Wide Ruin

Meigs, Cornelia
For ages 11 and up:
    Clearing Weather, NH
    The Covered Bridge (1780, New England)
    Fair Wind to Virginia (Colonial)
  * *Invincible Louisa*, NM (Louisa May Alcott)
  * *Swift Rivers*, NH (post–Louisiana Purchase)
    The Two Arrows (18th-century Maryland)
    The Willow Whistle (Midwest pioneering)
    Wind in the Chimney (post–American Revolution)
    Windy Hill, NH

Miller, Helen Markley
>   For ages 12 and up:
>> *Julie*
>> *Kirsti*
>> *The Long Valley*
>> *The Lucky Lacys*
>> *Promenade All*
>> *Sagebrush Ranch*

Montgomery, L. M.
>   For ages 10 and up:
>> * *The Blue Castle*
>> * *Jane of Lantern Hill*
>   The Anne of Green Gables series:
>> * *Anne of Green Gables*
>> * *Anne of Avonlea*
>> * *Chronicles of Avonlea*
>> * *Anne of the Island*
>> * *Anne's House of Dreams*
>> * *Rainbow Valley*
>> * *Further Chronicles of Avonlea*
>> * *Rilla of Ingleside*
>> * *Anne of Windy Poplars*
>> * *Anne of Ingleside*
>   The Emily series:
>> * *Emily of New Moon*
>> * *Emily Climbs*
>> * *Emily's Quest*

Moody, Ralph
>   For ages 9 and up:
>> *Come On, Seabiscuit!*
>> *Kit Carson and the Wild Frontier*
>> *Wells Fargo*

Morey, Walter
>   For ages 11 and up:
>> *Angry Waters*
>> * *Canyon Winter*

* *Deep Trouble*
* *Gentle Ben*
* *Gloomy Gus*
* *Home Is the North*
* *Kavik, the Wolf Dog*
* *Run Far, Run Fast*
* *Runaway Stallion*
* *Sandy and the Rock Star*
* *Scrub Dog of Alaska*
* *Year of the Black Pony*

Morrison, Lucile
> For ages 12 and up:
>> *The Lost Queen of Egypt*

Mowat, Farley
> For ages 9 and up:
>> * *Owls in the Family*
> For ages 11 and up:
>> *The Black Joke*
>> *The Curse of the Viking Grave* (sequel to *Lost in the Barrens*)
>> * *Lost in the Barrens*

Nesbit, E.
> For ages 10 and up:
>> * *The Railway Children*

Neville, Emily
> For ages 12 and up:
>> *Berries Goodman*
>> * *It's Like This, Cat*, NM

Nordhoff, Charles
> For ages 12 and up:
>> *Pearl Lagoon*

North, Sterling
> For ages 11 and up:
>> *Captured by the Mohawks*

      * *Rascal: A Memoir of a Better Era*
      So Dear to My Heart
      * *The Wolfling*

O'Brien, Robert C.
For ages 10 and up:
    * *Mrs. Frisby and the Rats of NIMH*, NM

Ottley, Reginald
For ages 11 and up:
    Giselle
Outback trilogy:
    Boy Alone
    The Roan Colt
    Rain Comes to Yamboorah

Parkinson, Ethelyn M.
For ages 9 to 14:
    The Operation That Happened to Rupert Piper
    The Terrible Troubles of Rupert Piper
    Rupert Piper and Megan, the Valuable Girl
    Rupert Piper and the Boy Who Could Knit
    Rupert Piper and the Dear Dear Birds

Paterson, Katherine
For ages 14 and up:
    * *Jacob Have I Loved*, NM

Pauli, Hertha
For ages 9 to 14:
    Two Trumpeters of Vienna (1683, Vienna)

Peart, Hendri
For ages 10 and up:
    Red Falcons of Trémoine

Pease, Howard
For ages 10 and up:
    Captain of the "Araby"

The Jinx Ship
Long Wharf (California Gold Rush)
Secret Cargo
The Tatooed Man
Thunderbolt House (1906, San Francisco)

Pederson, Elsa

For ages 12 and up:
Cook Inlet Decision
Dangerous Flight
Fisherman's Choice
House upon a Rock

Pellowski, Anne

For ages 9 and up:
The Farm series:
* *First Farm in the Valley: Anna's Story* (1870s)
* *Winding Valley Farm: Annie's Story* (early 1900s)
Stairstep Farm: Anna Rose's Story (1930s)
Willow Wind Farm: Betsy's Story (1960s)
Betsy's Up and Down Year (1960s)

Phipson, Joan

For ages 10 and up:
The Boundary Riders
Cross Currents
Good Luck to the Rider
The Barker series:
The Family Conspiracy
Threat to the Barkers

Picard, Barbara Leonie

For ages 12 and up:
One Is One (14th-century England)
Ransom for a Knight (14th-century England)

Polland, Madeleine

For ages 9 to 14:
Beorn the Proud (9th-century Ireland)

      Children of the Red King (Ireland and Norman Invasion)
      Chuiraquimba and the Black Robes (1600s, Paraguay)
      City of the Golden House (Nero's Rome)
   * *Fingal's Quest* (6th-century Gaul)
      The Queen's Blessing (St. Margaret of Scotland)
      Stranger in the Hills

Pope, Ray

For ages 10 and up:
   Salvage from Strosa
   Strosa Light

Porter, Gene Stratton

For ages 12 and up:
  * *Freckles*
  * *A Girl of the Limberlost*

Rankin, Louise

For ages 10 and up:
  * *Daughter of the Mountains*, NH

Ransome, Arthur

For ages 10 and up:
 The Swallows and Amazons series:
  * *Swallows and Amazons*
  * *Swallowdale*
  * *Peter Duck*
  * *Winter Holiday*
  * *Coot Club*
  * *Pigeon Post*
  * *We Didn't Mean to Go to Sea*
  * *Secret Water*
    The Big Six
    Missee Lee

Ray, Mary

For ages 12 and up:
   The Eastern Beacon
   The Spring Tide

The Hylas series:
>   *The Ides of April* (Rome of Nero)
>   *Beyond the Desert Gate* (Jewish revolt against Rome)
>   *Rain from the West* (Roman Britain)

Reilly, Robert T.

For ages 10 and up:
>   *Massacre at Ash Hollow*
>   * *Red Hugh, Prince of Donegal*

Reiss, Johanna

For ages 12 and up:
>   * *The Journey Back* (sequel to *Upstairs Room*)
>   * *The Upstairs Room*, NH (World War II)

Riesenberg, Jr., Felix

For ages 11 and up:
>   *The Mysterious Sailor*

Ritchie, Rita

For ages 10 and up:
>   *The Enemy at the Gate* (1529, Seige of Vienna)
>   *The Golden Hawks of Genghis Khan*
>   *Secret beyond the Mountains*
>   *The Year of the Horse*

Rushmore, Helen

For ages 12 and up:
>   *Shadow of Robber's Roost*

Savery, Constance

For ages 10 and up:
>   *Dark House on the Moss*
>   *Enemy Brothers* (World War II)
>   *Magic in My Shoes*
>   *Moonshine in Candle Street*
>   *Pippin's House*
>   *The Reb and the Redcoats* (American Revolution)
>   *Welcome, Santza*

Sawyer, Ruth
> For ages 11 and up:
>> * *Roller Skates*, NM
>> *The Year of Jubilo* (sequel to *Roller Skates*)

Schaefer, Jack Warner
> For ages 12 and up:
>> *Old Ramon*, NH
>> * *Shane*

Seredy, Kate (author and illustrator)
> For ages 10 and up:
>> *The Chestry Oak*
>> * *The Good Master*, NH
>> *Philomena*
>> * *The Singing Tree* (sequel to *The Good Master*)
>> * *The White Stag*, NM

Serraillier, Ian
> For ages 10 and up:
>> * *Escape from Warsaw* (also entitled *The Silver Sword*)

Shemin, Margaretha
> For ages 12 and up:
>> *The Empty Moat*

Smith, C. Fox
> For ages 11 and up:
>> *The Ship Aground*

Smith, Dodie
> For ages 9 and up:
>> * *The Hundred and One Dalmatians*
>> *The Starlight Barking: More about the Hundred and One Dalmatians*

Smith, Emma

For ages 11 and up:
  No Way of Telling
  Out of Hand

Smucker, Barbara

For ages 11 and up:
  Amish Adventure
  Days of Terror
  * *Incredible Jumbo*
  * *Runaway to Freedom: A Story of the Underground Railroad*

Snedeker, Caroline Dale

For ages 9 to 14:
  Theras and His Town
For ages 12 and up:
  The Beckoning Road (sequel to *Downright Dency*)
  Downright Dency, NH (19th-century Nantucket Island)
  The Forgotten Daughter, NH (Greek slave in Rome)
  Luke's Quest
  The Perilous Seat (Ancient Greece)
  The White Isle (Roman Britain)

Sobol, Donald J.

For ages 10 and up:
  Secret Agents Four

Speare, Elizabeth George

For ages 10 and up:
  * *The Sign of the Beaver*, NH
For ages 12 and up:
  * *The Bronze Bow*, NM
  * *Calico Captive* (18th-century New England)
  * *The Witch of Blackbird Pond*, NM (17th-century Connecticut)

Sperry, Armstrong (author and illustrator)

For ages 10 and up:
  All Sail Set: A Romance of the Flying Cloud, NH
  * *Call It Courage*, NM

Danger to Windward
Hull-Down for Action
Wagons Westward: The Old Trail to Santa Fe

Spyri, Johanna
For ages 9 and up:
* * Heidi*
Moni, the Goat Boy
The Pet Lamb
Veronica
Vinzi

Stevenson, Robert Louis
For ages 9 and up:
* * David Balfour*
* * Kidnapped*
* * Treasure Island*

Streatfeild, Noel
For ages 10 and up:
* * Ballet Shoes*, CMH
The Circus Is Coming, CM
Dancing Shoes
The Family at Caldicott Place
Family Shoes
Gemma
Gemma Alone
Gemma and Sisters
Goodbye Gemma
The Magic Summer
Movie Shoes
New Shoes
Party Shoes
Skating Shoes
Tennis Shoes, CMH
Theater Shoes
Thursday's Child
Traveling Shoes
When the Sirens Wailed

Styles, Showell

For ages 10 and up:
Journey with a Secret
Sherpa Adventure

The Midshipman Quinn series:
Midshipman Quinn
Quinn of the "Fury"
Quinn at Trafalgar
Midshipman Quinn Wins Through
Midshipman Quinn and Denise the Spy

The Simon and Mag series:
The Shop in the Mountains
The Ladder of Snow
The Pass of Morning

Sutcliff, Rosemary

For ages 11 and up:
Dawnwind (6th-century Britain)
Knight's Fee (11th-century Britain)
* *Outcast* (2d-century Britain/Rome)
The Shield Ring, CH (11th-century Britain)
* *Warrior Scarlet*, CH (Bronze Age Britain)

Roman Britain Trilogy:
* *The Eagle of the Ninth*, CH
* *The Lantern Bearers*, CM
* *The Silver Branch*, CH

Taylor, Don Alonzo

For ages 11 and up:
Old Sam and the Horse Thieves
Old Sam, Thoroughbred Trotter

Taylor, Sydney

For ages 8 and up:
A Papa Like Everyone Else

The All-of-a-Kind Family series:
All-of-a-Kind Family
More All-of-a-Kind Family
All-of-a-Kind Family Downtown

All-of-a-Kind Family Uptown
Ella of All-of-a-Kind Family

Taylor, Theodore
For ages 10 and up:
* The Cay
* Timothy of the Cay: A Prequel-Sequel

Tolkien, J. R. R.
For ages 9 and up:
* The Hobbit

Travers, P. L.
For ages 10 and up:
I Go by Sea, I Go by Land (World War II)

Trease, Geoffrey
For ages 10 and up:
The Barons' Hostage: A Story of Simon de Montfort (13th century)
Message to Hadrian (2d century-Rome/Britain)
No Boats on Bannermere
Red Towers of Granada (13th century)
The Secret Fiord (15th-century Britain/Norway)
Trumpets in the West
Victory at Valmy (French Revolution)
Web of Traitors: An Adventure Story of Ancient Athens

Treviño, Elizabeth
For ages 12 and up:
I, Juan de Pareja, NM

Trevor, Meriol
For ages 10 and up:
Lights in a Dark Town
* The Rose Round
The Sparrow Child
Sun Slower, Sun Faster

The Letzenstein Chronicles:
  * *The Crystal Snowstorm*
  * *Following the Phoenix*
    Angel and Dragon
    The Rose and Crown

Tunis, John
  For ages 11 and up:
    Silence over Dunkerque (World War II)

Turner, Philip
  For ages 12 and up:
  The Darnley Mills series:
    Devil's Nob
    Steam on the Line
    Colonel Sheperton's Clock
    Powder Quay
    The Grange at High Force, CM
    Sea Peril
    War on the Darnel

Turngren, Ellen
  For ages 14 and up:
    Hearts Are the Fields (sequel to *Shadows into Mist*)
    Listen, My Heart
    Shadows into Mist

Ullman, James Ramsey
  For ages 11 and up:
  * *Banner in the Sky*, NH

Van Stockum, Hilda (author and illustrator)
  For ages 9 and up:
  * *Andries*
    Gerrit and the Organ
  * *The Winged Watchman*

The Bantry Bay series:
* * *The Cottage at Bantry Bay*
* * *Francie on the Run*
* * *Pegeen*
The Mitchells series:
* * *The Mitchells: Five for Victory*
* * *Canadian Summer*
* * *Friendly Gables*
For ages 12 and up:
> *The Borrowed House*
> *Penengro*

Vipont, Elfrida
For ages 12 and up:
> *Flowering Spring*
> *The Lark in the Morn*
> *The Lark on the Wing*, CM (sequel to *Lark in the Morn*)
> *The Pavilion*
> *The Spring of the Year*

Wallace, Sr. M. Imelda
For ages 10 to 14:
* * *Outlaws of Ravenhurst*

Watson, Sally
For ages 14 and up:
> *Other Sandals* (sequel to *To Build a Land*)
> *To Build a Land* (1947, Israel)

Webster, Jean
For ages 11 and up:
* * *Daddy-Long-Legs*
> *Dear Enemy*

Weir, Rosemary
For ages 10 and up:
> *High Courage* (Simon de Montfort)
> *The Lion and the Rose* (St. Paul's Cathedral)
> *The Real Game*

The Star and the Flame (Fire of London)
Summer of the Silent Hands

Welch, Ronald

For ages 14 and up:
Bowman of Crécy (Hundred Years' War)
The Carey family historical series:
Knight Crusader, CM (12th century)
The Hawk (Elizabethan)
For the King (English Civil War)
Captain of Dragoons (17th century)
Mohawk Valley (Fall of Quebec)
Escape from France (French Revolution)
Nicholas Carey (Crimean War)
Tank Commander (World War I)

Werstein, Irving

For ages 11 and up:
The Long Escape (Belgium, World War II)

Whelan, Gloria

For ages 10 and up:
* *Forgive the River, Forgive the Sky*
* *Goodbye, Vietnam*
* *Once on This Island* (War of 1812)
* *That Wild Berries Should Grow*
* *A Time to Keep Silent*

White, E. B.

For ages 9 and up:
* *Charlotte's Web*
* *Stuart Little*

White, Robb

For ages 12 and up:
* *Deathwatch*
  Flight Deck (World War II)
  The Frogmen (World War II)

The Lion's Paw
A Long Way Down
Secret Sea
Silent Ship, Silent Sea (World War II)
Surrender! (Philippines, World War II)
The Survivor (World War II)
Torpedo Run (World War II)
Up Periscope (World War II)

Wibberley, Leonard
For ages 11 and up:
  * *Flint's Island*
The Treegate series (pre–American Revolution through the War of 1812):
  * *John Treegate's Musket*
    Peter Treegate's War
    Sea Captain from Salem
    Treegate's Raiders
    Leopard's Prey
    Red Pawns
    The Last Battle
As **Patrick O'Connor**:
    The Black Tiger
    Black Tiger at Bonneville
    Black Tiger at Indianapolis
    Black Tiger at Le Mans
    The Lost Harpooner
    Mexican Road Race
    Treasure at Twenty Fathoms
As **Christopher Webb**:
    Matt Tyler's Chronicle
    The Quest of the Otter

Wier, Ester
For ages 11 and up:
    The Barrel
    Gift of the Mountains
    King of the Mountains

* *The Loner*, NH
  The Long Year
  The Rumptydoolers
  The Straggler
  The Wind Chasers
  The Winners

Wiggin, Kate Douglas
For ages 10 and up:
* *New Chronicles of Rebecca*
* *Rebecca of Sunnybrook Farm*

Wilder, Laura Ingalls
For ages 9 and up:
The Little House series:
* *Little House in the Big Woods*
* *Little House on the Prairie*
* *On the Banks of Plum Creek*, NH
* *By the Shores of Silver Lake*, NH
* *The Long Winter*, NH
* *Little Town on the Prairie*, NH
* *Farmer Boy*

* *These Happy Golden Years*, NH
* *The First Four Years*
For ages 12 and up:
* *On the Way Home: The Diary of a Trip from South Dakota to Mansfield, Missouri, in 1894* (written with **Rose Wilder Lane**)
* *West from Home: Letters from Laura Ingalls Wilder to Almanzo Wilder, San Francisco, 1915* (ed. by **Roger Lea MacBride**)

Willard, Barbara
For ages 10 and 14:
* *Augustine Came to Kent*
  Flight to the Forest
  If All the Swords in England
* *Son of Charlemagne*

> *Storm from the West*
For ages 12 and up:
The Mantlemass series:
> *The Lark and the Laurel*
> *The Sprig of Broom*
> *A Cold Wind Blowing*
> *The Iron Lily*
> *Harrow and Harvest*
> *The Miller's Boy*
> *The Eldest Son*
> *A Flight of Swans*
> *The Keys of Mantlemass*

Williamson, Joanne

For ages 11 and up:
> *The Eagles Have Flown* (Rome at the time of Julius Caesar's death)
> *The Glorious Conspiracy* (English mills and New York politics during the Federalist period)
> *The Hittite Warrior* (biblical times of Deborah and Barak)

Wormser, Richard

For ages 12 and up:
> *The Black Mustanger*
> *Gone to Texas*
> *Ride a Northbound Horse*

Worth, Katherine

For ages 12 and up:
> *New Worlds for Josie*
> * *They Loved to Laugh* (Quaker family in the 1830s)

Wuorio, Eva-Lis

For ages 12 and up:
> *Code: Polonaise* (Poland, World War II)
> *To Fight in Silence* (Denmark, World War II)
> *October Treasure* (Channel Islands)
> *Venture at Midsummer* (Finland, sequel to *October Treasure*)

Yates, Elizabeth

For ages 11 and up:

* * *Amos Fortune, Free Man*, NM
* * *Mountain Born*, NH
* * *The Next Fine Day*
* * *A Place for Peter* (sequel to *Mountain Born*)

For ages 12 and up:

* * *Hue and Cry* (sequel to *The Journeyman*)
* * *The Journeyman*
* * *Prudence Crandall, Woman of Courage*
* * *Someday You'll Write*
* * *Sound Friendships*
  With Pipe, Paddle, and Song

THREE EXCELLENT SERIES BY DIFFERENT AUTHORS

Land of the Free Series

For ages 12 and up:

Door to the North: A Saga of 14th Century America, written by **Elizabeth Coatsworth**

Footprints of the Dragon, written by **Vanya Oakes** (Chinese and the Pacific Railways)

I Heard of a River, written by **Elsie Singmaster** (Germans in Pennsylvania)

The Last Fort: A Story of the French Voyagers, written by **Elizabeth Coatsworth**

Seek the Dark Gold, written by **Jo Evalin Lundy** (Scots fur traders)

Seven Bear Skins, written by **Erick Berry** (Dutch in New Amsterdam)

The Sign of the Golden Fish, written by **Gertrude Robinson** (Cornish fisherman in Maine)

Song of the Pines, written by **Walter and Marion Havighurst** (Norwegian lumbering in Wisconsin), NH

Tidewater Valley, written by **Jo Evalin Lundy** (Swiss dairy farmers in Oregon)

Reissued Scribner Illustrated Classics

For ages 10 and up:

Books illustrated by **N. C. Wyeth**:

* *The Boy's King Arthur*, written by **Sidney Lanier**
* *David Balfour*, written by **Robert Louis Stevenson**
* *The Deerslayer*, written by **James Fenimore Cooper**
* *Drums*, written by **James Boyd**
* *Kidnapped*, written by **Robert Louis Stevenson**
* *The Last of the Mohicans*, written by **James Fenimore Cooper**
* *The Mysterious Island*, written by **Jules Verne**
* *Robin Hood*, written by **Paul Creswick**
* *Robinson Crusoe*, written by **Daniel Defoe**
* *The Scottish Chiefs*, written by **Jane Porter**
* *Treasure Island*, written by **Robert Louis Stevenson**
* *Westward Ho!*, written by **Charles Kingsley**
* *The Yearling*, written by **Marjorie Kinnan Rawlings**

Books illustrated by **Maxfield Parrish**:

* *The Arabian Nights*, edited by **Kate Douglas Wiggin** and **Nora A. Smith**

Vision Books

For ages 9 and up:

* *The Curé of Ars: The Priest Who Out-talked the Devil*, written by **Milton Lomask**
* *Edmund Campion: Hero of God's Underground*, written by **Harold Gardiner, S.J.**
* *Father Marquette and the Great Rivers*, written by **August Derleth**
* *Francis and Clare: Saints of Assisi*, written by **Helen Homan**
* *Kateri Tekakwitha: Mohawk Maid*, written by **Evelyn Brown**
* *St. Dominic and the Rosary*, written by **Catherine Beebe**
* *St. Francis and the Seven Seas*, written by **Albert J. Nevins, M.M.**
* *St. Isaac and the Indians*, written by **Milton Lomask**
* *St. John Bosco and St. Dominic Savio*, written by **Catherine Beebe**

ADULT TITLES

The following consists of books originally written for adults but which are suitable for older teens. We still assume parents will be making final decisions about what is appropriate for their child. At the end of the list are brief World War II and Classic Mystery sections.

Aldrich, Bess Streeter
* *A Lantern in Her Hand*

Austin, Jane
* *Emma*
* *Mansfield Park*
* *Northanger Abbey*
* *Persuasion*
* *Pride and Prejudice*
* *Sense and Sensibility*

Barrett, William
* *The Lilies of the Field*

Belloc, Hilaire
* *The Bad Child's Book of Beasts*
  More Beasts (for Worse Children): Verses
  A Moral Alphabet
  Cautionary Tales for Children: Designed for the Admonition of Children between the Ages of Eight and Fourteen Years: Verses
  New Cautionary Tales: Verses

Benson, Msgr. Hugh
* *The Lord of the World*

Bjorn, Thyra Ferré
* *Mama's Way*

* *Papa's Daughter* (sequel to *Papa's Wife*)
* *Papa's Wife*

Blackmore, R. D.
* *Lorna Doone*

Brontë, Charlotte
* *Jane Eyre*

Broster, D. K.
Ships in the Bay!
The Jacobite trilogy:
The Flight of the Heron
The Dark Mile
The Gleam of the North

Buchan, John
* *John McNab*
* *Prester John*
* *Witch Wood*
The Dickson McCunn series:
* *Huntingtower*
* *Castle Gay*
The Richard Hannay series:
* *The Thirty-Nine Steps*
* *Greenmantle*
* *Mr. Standfast*
The Power House
* *The Three Hostages*
* *The Island of Sheep*

Cather, Willa
* *Death Comes for the Archbishop*
* *My Antonia*
* *Shadows on the Rock*

Chesterton, G. K.
* *The Ballad of the White Horse*
* *The Ball and the Cross*

   * *The Father Brown Omnibus*
   The Flying Inn
   Manalive
   * *The Man Who Was Thursday*
   * *The Napoleon of Notting Hill*

Childers, Erskine
   * *The Riddle of the Sands*

Clark, Isabel C.
   A Case of Conscience
   Children of the Shadow
   and others . . .

Coatsworth, Elizabeth
   Here I Stay: A Maine Novel

Cooper, James Fenimore
   * *The Deerslayer*
   * *The Last of the Mohicans*

Dana, Richard
   * *Two Years before the Mast*

De Wohl, Louis
   * *Citadel of God: A Novel about Saint Benedict*
   * *Lay Siege to Heaven: A Novel about Saint Catherine of Siena*
   * *The Quiet Light: A Novel about Saint Thomas Aquinas*
   * *The Restless Flame: A Novel about Saint Augustine*
   * *Set All Afire: A Novel about Saint Francis Xavier*
   * *The Spear* (about Longinus)

Doyle, Sir Arthur Conan
   * *The Lost World*
   * *The White Company*
   * The Sherlock Holmes stories

Erdman, Loula Grace
   * *The Edge of Time*

> *The Years of the Locust*
> *Lonely Passage*

Forbes, Kathryn
> * *Mama's Bank Account*

Gilbreth, Jr., Frank B. and **Ernestine Gilbreth Carey**
> * *Belles on Their Toes*
> * *Cheaper by the Dozen*

Godden, Rumer
> *The Dark Horse*
> * *In This House of Brede*

Goldsmith, Oliver
> * *The Vicar of Wakefield*

Goudge, Elizabeth
> * *The Bird in the Tree*
> * *A City of the Bells*
> * *Dean's Watch*
> *Green Dolphin Street*
> * *Heart of the Family*
> *Pilgrim's Inn*
> * *The Rosemary Tree*
> *The Scent of Water*

Graham, Robin Lee, with **Derek Gill**
> * *Dove*

Haggard, Henry Rider
> * *Allan Quatermain*
> * *King Solomon's Mines*
> * *She*

Hemon, Louis
> * *Maria Chapdelaine*, illus. by **Clarence Gagnon**

Herriot, James
 The James Herriot series:
  * *All Creatures Great and Small*
  * *All Things Wise and Wonderful*
  * *All Things Bright and Beautiful*
  * *The Lord God Made Them All*
  * *Every Living Thing*

Hilton, James
  * *Goodbye, Mr. Chips*

Hope-Hawkins, Anthony
  * *The Prisoner of Zenda*

Hugo, Victor
  * *Les Miserables*

Keller, Helen
  * *The Story of My Life*

Kipling, Rudyard
  * *Captains Courageous*

Lee, Harper
  * *To Kill a Mockingbird*

Lewis, C. S.
  * *Out of the Silent Planet*
  * *Perelandra*
  * *That Hideous Strength*

Magnusson, Sally
  * *The Flying Scotsman*

Marshall, Catherine
  * *Christy*

Merrill, Jean
  * *The Pushcart War*

Moody, Ralph
The Little Britches series:
* *Little Britches*
* *Man of the Family*
* *The Fields of Home*
* *The Home Ranch*
* *Mary Emma and Company*
* *Shaking the Nickel Bush*
* *The Dry Divide*
* *Horse of a Different Color*

Nordhoff, Charles
* *Mutiny on the Bounty*

O'Hara, Mary
The My Friend Flicka series:
* *My Friend Flicka*
* *Thunderhead*
  The Green Grass of Wyoming

Orczy, Baroness
* *The Scarlet Pimpernel*

Patton, Frances Gray
  Good Morning, Miss Dove

Portis, Charles
* *True Grit*

Potok, Chaim
* *The Chosen*
* *The Promise*

Sabatini, Rafael
* *Captain Blood*
* *Scaramouche*
* *The Sea Hawk*

Shellabarger, Samuel
   Prince of Foxes

Sienkiewicz, Henryk
   * *Quo Vadis?*

Tolkien, J. R. R.
   * *The Lord of the Rings*
   * *The Silmarillion*

Trapp, Maria Augusta
   Around the Year with the Trapp Family
   * *The Story of the Trapp Family Singers*

Trevor, Meriol
   Shadows and Images

Twain, Mark
   * *Joan of Arc*

Verne, Jules
   A Long Vacation (originally entitled *A Two Years' Vacation*)
   * *Michael Strogoff: The Courier of the Czar*
   * *The Mysterious Island*
   * *Twenty Thousand Leagues under the Sea*

Wibberley, Leonard
   Epics of Everest
   The Hands of Cormac Joyce
   The Land That Isn't There: An Irish Adventure
   The Last Stand of Father Felix
   The Shannon Sailors: A Voyage to the Heart of Ireland
   The Mouse series:
   * *Beware of the Mouse!*
   * *The Mouse That Roared*
   The Mouse on the Moon
   The Mouse on Wall Street
   The Mouse That Saved the West

As **Leonard Holton**:
The Father Bredder mysteries

Wister, Owen
* *The Virginian*

Wodehouse, P. G.
* *French Leave*
* *Heavy Weather*
* *Laughing Gas*
* *Man Upstairs and Other Stories*
* *Something Fresh*
* *Summer Lightning*

Wren, Percival
* *Beau Geste*

WORLD WAR II BOOKS

Brickhill, Paul
* *The Great Escape*

Burgess, Alan
The Small Woman

Gordon, Ernest
Through the Valley of the Kwai

Hersey, John
* *Hiroshima*
Of Men and War

Olsen, Oluf Reed
Assignment: Spy (originally titled *Two Eggs on My Plate*)

Reid, Pat
Escape from Colditz

Ryan, Cornelius
  * *The Longest Day*

Ten Boom, Corrie
  * *The Hiding Place*

Trumbull, Robert
  * *The Raft*

Williams, Eric
  * *The Wooden Horse*

CLASSIC BRITISH AND AMERICAN MURDER MYSTERIES

Allingham, Margery
  * *Black Plumes*
  * *Fashion in Shrouds*
  * *More Work for the Undertaker*
  * *Pearls before Swine*
  * *Tether's End*
  * *Tiger in the Smoke*
  * *Traitor's Purse*

Bentley, E. C.
  * *Trent's Last Case*

Biggers, Earl Derr
    Behind That Curtain
  * *The Black Camel*
  * *Charlie Chan Carries On*
    The Chinese Parrot
  * *The House without a Key*
    Keeper of the Keys

Collins, Wilkie
  * *The Moonstone*
  * *The Woman in White*

Sayers, Dorothy
  * *The Documents in the Case*
  * *Gaudy Night*
  * *Have His Carcase*
  * *Lord Peter*
  * *Murder Must Advertise*
  * *The Nine Tailors*
  * *Strong Poison*
  * *Unnatural Death*
  * *The Unpleasantness at the Bellona Club*
  * *Whose Body?*

Tey, Josephine
  * *The Daughter of Time*
  * *The Franchise Affair*
  * *The Singing Sands*

White, Ethel Lina
  The Lady Vanishes